Dear Reader:

The book you are about to read is the latest bestseller from St. Martin's True Crime Library, the imprint *The New York Times* calls "the leader in true crime!" Each month, we offer you a fascinating account of the latest, most sensational crime that has captured national attention. *The Milwaukee Murders* delves into the twisted world of Jeffrey Dahmer, one of the most savage serial killers of our time; *Lethal Lolita* gives you the *real* scoop on the deadly love affair between Amy Fisher and Joey Buttafuoco; *Whoever Fights Monsters* takes you inside the special FBI team that tracks serial killers; *Garden of Graves* reveals how police uncovered the bloody human harvest of mass murderer Joel Rifkin; *Unanswered Cries* is the story of a detective who tracked a killer for a year, only to discover it was someone he knew and trusted; *Bad Blood* is the story of the notorious Menendez brothers and their sensational trials; *Sins of the Mother* details the sad account of Susan Smith and her two drowned children; *Fallen Hero* details the riveting tragedy of O. J. Simpson and the case that stunned a nation.

St. Martin's True Crime Library gives you the stories *behind* the headlines. Our authors take you right to the scene of the crime and into the minds of the most notorious murderers to show you what really makes them tick. St. Martin's True Crime Library paperbacks are better than the most terrifying thriller, because it's all true! The next time you want a crackling good read, make sure it's got the St. Martin's True Crime Library logo on the spine—you'll be up all night!

Charles E. Spicer, Jr.

Charles E. Spicer, Jr.
Senior Editor, St. Martin's True Crime Library

The young man with the tousled black hair lounged at the pay telephone stall, oblivious to the other man at the adjacent phone who was pretending to make his own call.

"You ought to be down here," the young man said, to whoever it was on the other end of his line. "Both your parents and your sister. Give me the keys and we'll have a party at the house."

And then the young man laughed, while the hair rose on the back of the man standing next to him.

Cold, so cold, the undercover cop thought. These guys are really, really cold.

Also by Carlton Smith

DEATH OF A LITTLE PRINCESS
BLOOD MONEY

SEEDS of EVIL

CARLTON SMITH

St. Martin's Paperbacks

SEEDS OF EVIL

Copyright © 1997 by Carlton Smith.

Cover photographs by John Storey/People Weekly © 1995.

ISBN: 0-312-96285-1

Printed in the United States of America

St. Martin's Paperbacks edition/September 1997

10 9 8 7 6 5 4 3 2 1

AUTHOR'S NOTE AND ACKNOWLEDGMENTS

On Easter Sunday in 1992, an unknown gunman entered a house in Fresno, California, and methodically murdered an entire family.

From the positions of the dead—59-year-old Dale Ewell, his politically and socially prominent wife Glee Mitchell Ewell, and their 24-year-old daughter Tiffany—it was clear that someone had calmly slaughtered the Ewells one by one, just as they arrived at their comfortable middle-class house in southeast Fresno.

Why was the Ewell family targeted for death? And who did it? For nearly three years police labored to solve this often seemingly insoluble puzzle, spending several million dollars in public money and tens of thousands of man-hours in the process.

Motives abounded. Some said the Ewell murders were the work of mobsters or drug dealers, retaliating against Dale Ewell for past sins, real or imagined. Others claimed that Glee Ewell's CIA past had finally caught up with her. Still others theorized that the murders were somehow connected with the late Philippine dictator Ferdinand Marcos' still-mysterious missing millions, even as other rumors swirled suggesting that the killings were the work of a new Manson-style gang of death cultists, bent on preying upon the wealthy, a sort of Helter-Skelter for the nineties.

Then, to the shock of almost everyone, the Ewells' sole surviving son, Dana—a brilliant, 24-year-old magna cum laude graduate of Santa Clara University, who had been more than 100 miles away at the time the killings took place—was arrested and charged with hiring someone to wipe out his entire family. Dana's alleged motive was simple: it was greed, the police claimed.

Dana Ewell wanted, police said, to take over everything that his daddy had: Dale Ewell's businesses, his car, his money, his house, indeed, even his personality—right down to his briefcase. In short, police claimed, Dana Ewell wanted to *be* Dale Ewell. It was, they seemed to suggest, a macabre tragedy that seemed a grotesque collision between the Oedipus Complex and the Greed Decade.

And the cold-blooded killer allegedly hired by Dana Ewell to wipe out his father, mother, and sister?

None other than one of Dana Ewell's very best friends, like Dana, also a graduate of Santa Clara University, a school centered on every precept of Christian morality, and himself the son of a prominent Southern California aerospace engineer.

"What happened in that house?" the minister presiding over the Ewell family's funeral asked, a week after the murders, but long before Dana Ewell was arrested.

"Was it senseless, urban violence, or bizarre, twisted killings?"

There indeed was a profound question. However much we might choose to believe that homicidal violence has nothing to do with us, we are wrong. There is no cultural bar to murder, no income inoculation to its depredations. Urban or rural, sensible or senseless, bizarre or ordinary, all murder is twisted—especially to those who lose their lives.

This is the story of Dana Ewell, and his friend, Joel Radovcich. It is, in part, about the conditions of their lives—comfortable, even rich by most accounts—and it is about how they viewed their lives—their values.

It is about a handful of detectives who worked for more than three years to piece together a complex puzzle, whose solution even now is not yet clear.

And it is a story about the justice system, the way it works, or doesn't, sometimes maddeningly slow and seemingly arcane, caught in technical and legal minutiae that may seem infinitesimally petty—until you are the one accused.

At the time of this writing, the jury trial of Dana Ewell and Joel Radovcich has not yet been held. Inevitably, under those circumstances, it wasn't possible to get the whole story—after all, the whole story will come only when and if a jury decides whether Dana Ewell and Joel Radovcich are guilty of cold-blooded murder.

Until then, Dana Ewell and Joel Radovcich are innocent—as the phrase goes, innocent until proven guilty. Understandably, on the basis of advice from their legal counsel, neither Dana Ewell nor Joel Radovcich were willing to be interviewed for this book. Nor were a number of the police officers principally involved with the long investigation into the Ewell murders willing to discuss their work directly, or subject their conclusions to examination in advance of the trial.

It was, nevertheless, still possible to piece together the most important pieces of the puzzle.

Drawing on nearly 900 pages of preliminary hearing transcript, an additional 600 pages of court briefs, declarations, and pleadings, from documents filed in other legal proceedings, from newspaper accounts published in the *San Jose Mercury-News* and the *Fresno Bee*, from numerous interviews, and from other documents associated with the police investigation, it was possible to reconstruct most of the events that led to the sensational arrests of two young men who had everything, but who were said to want even more. . . .

No work such as this can be prepared without the generous assistance of people who are willing to patiently put up with interminable, often dumb questions, and such is the case here. The author gratefully acknowledges the assistance of Fresno County Sheriff Steve Magarian, Fresno County District Attorney Ed Hunt, Chief Criminal Deputy District Attorney Jim Oppliger, Chief Public Defender Peter Jones, and Fresno County Chief Criminalist Allen Boudreau, along with Fresno attorneys Michael Dowling and Curtis Sisk, in developing much of the information included in this book. Appreciation is also extended to Margo St. James and Carol Stuart of San Francisco, and Daryl and Martha Troedson of Southern California, for their support; and last but hardly least, to Rod and Era of Tiny's, Fresno's home-away-from-home, on the highway known as Ninety-nine.

Carlton Smith
San Francisco, 1996

KEY TO MAP

People:

K1   Killer enters master bedroom, obtains 9-mm ammunition

K2   Killer waits in laundry room

K3   On hearing Tiffany and Glee enter from garage, killer exits laundry room for kitchen, shoots Tiffany in the back of the head, TE

K4   Killer confronts Glee in hall outside office, GE1

K5   Killer shoots Glee in the office, GE2

K6   Killer waits for Dale Ewell in Dana's bedroom

K7   Killer shoots Dale Ewell in back of the neck in the hallway, DE

B1   Spent bullet recovered from under Glee's left shoulder

B2   Spent bullet recovered under Glee's head

B3   Spent bullet recovered from wall

B4   Spent bullet recovered from outside flower bed

B5   Spent bullet recovered from kitchen wall

M=   Rooms with motion detectors

Evidence Observed:

E1   sheet, stereo, CDs, costume jewelry, camera found in entry hall bathroom

E2   television unplugged, removed from shelf, open drawers, cabinets, clothing on floor

E3   bedding removed, drawers opened, bedside cabinet opened, ammunition disturbed, handgun missing, loose 9-mm ammunition

E4   Beneath Dale's body, a newspaper, a magazine, mail, a fax, broken sunglasses

E5   Near Glee Ewell, her keys

E6   Near Tiffany Ewell, a music casette, a sweatshirt, a soft-drink cup

E7   On kitchen table, an ice cooler, a woman's jacket, Glee's purse

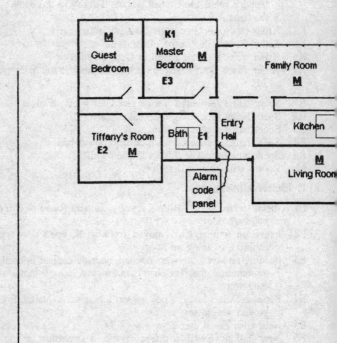

5663 East Park Circle

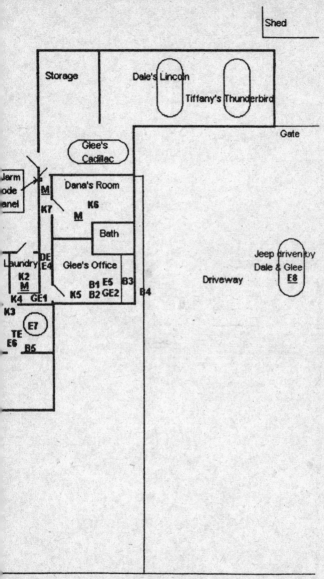

Shed

Storage

Dale's Lincoln

Tiffany's Thunderbird

Gate

Glee's
Cadillac

Alarm
Code
Panel

M

Dana's Room

K7

M

K6

M

Bath

Laundry

DE
E4

Glee's Office

K2
M

B1 E5 B3
B2 GE2

K4 GE1

K5

K3

TE
E6

E7

B4

B5

Jeep driven by
Dale & Glee
E8

Driveway

Drive

PROLOGUE

The shift was nearing its end; no one paid much attention to the old piece of equipment in the darkest reaches of the Winchester ammunition plant in East Alton, Illinois.

Forty times a minute, once every 1.6 seconds, the coning punch came down, crimping the copper jacket around the base of the bullet so that another punch could force the copper flat across the lead core an instant later. Bullets, thousands of them every hour, were dressed for fitting into the 9-millimeter cartridge cases that the Winchester company had decided to make for a still-uncertain market.

The year was 1971. Nine-millimeter ammunition was then a sideline for Winchester, nothing to compare to the vast numbers of .223-caliber rounds the company was then making for the U.S. Army, and the war then still raging, 12,000 miles away. Nine-millimeter rounds were a specialty item, for European weapons mainly, and as the worn-out coning punch labored on, no one noticed that it was producing jackets that were less than perfect.

At length, after being mated to the shiny brass cartridge cases filled with gunpowder, then sorted and segregated and automatically packaged in small cardboard boxes, fifty rounds each, the flawed 9-millimeter bullets manufactured at East Alton were shipped from the factory: first to Chicago, then Los Angeles, and eventually, to Fresno, California, where, in the fall of 1971, a man named Dale Ewell walked into a place called Sunnyside Hardware and purchased a Browning 9-millimeter, semiautomatic pistol and two boxes of the ammunition.

Dale Ewell was then 36 years old; he had a wife, Glee, a 3-year-old daughter, Tiffany, and a 9-month-old son, Dana. He also had a problem: his employer, an aircraft dealer, had just been arrested and accused of smuggling drugs.

Who knew what might happen? Dale Ewell's boss was said to have unsavory connections; the boss was going to prison, Dale knew that from the minute the federal agents had arrived at the offices one afternoon, telling him to take whatever was his from his desk and clear out, because Frank Lambe Aviation was, from that minute on, closed; and Dale, a hardened realist if there ever was one, knew that Frank had both friends and enemies who might believe, however erroneously, that Frank Lambe's chief salesman might know a little too much for anyone's comfort.

A Browning 9-millimeter pistol, with suitable ammunition, Dale Ewell thought, might be a prudent thing for his family to have around. . . .

OPENING GAMBIT

1

For most drivers heading north or south through California's long Central Valley, Fresno is a place to pass through, a spot on the long, melting asphalt ribbon of U.S. 99, made discernible only by the quickening of exits, the dim shapes of larger buildings to the east, and a sudden but suppressible yearning to take the Highway 41 cutoff for Yosemite before the off-ramp flits by, too late for reconsideration.

The main thing is the road, baking in the heat—mostly two lanes in each direction, a road from the fifties linking the two ends of the nation's longest state. It is dry farm country, this valley: mainly cotton, olives, almonds, pecans, pistachios, occasionally a patch of corn, but still the richest agricultural land in the nation. The fields reel away from the roadside, receding into the hot, hazy distance—the gray-greens of miles upon miles of neatly planted olive groves, the brighter green of the nut trees, yellowed grass of an endless plain of pasturage, broken only occasionally by a battered wooden barn or shed, an occasional turn-of-the century farmhouse set off by a stout and rounded palm, planted when Roosevelt—Teddy that is—was president.

In the distance to the east rises the rampart of the Sierra Nevada Mountains, vaguely bluish in the haze, but promising the cooler climes of higher elevation, and offering its life-giving supply of cold ice-melt water rushing down from its canyons—the Kern, the Tulare, the San Joaquin, the King.

Before the highway, of course, was the railroad; and it is to Leland Stanford and the Southern Pacific that the city of Fresno owes its existence. In 1872, Stanford, a former California governor and founder of the transcontinental railroad that eventually evolved into the Southern Pacific—"the Octopus," as it was later called by social reformers—was making a trip through the southeastern part of the vast San Joaquin Valley when he came upon nearly two thousand acres planted in ripe, golden wheat, and watered by the precious Sierra snowmelt. Here, Stanford decided, was the ideal route for his railroad's line south to Los Angeles and the vast markets he envisioned for that city's future.

In those days, the county seat was in Visalia, thirty miles to the southeast. Fresno County, as it was called for the Spanish word for ash tree, was a dry, desert region of low watercourses lined by the ubiquitous ash and willow, along with plains of yellowed grass, punctuated by patches of prickly pear. In summer the heat was searing, while in winter, the fog lay cold and clammy, close to the earth; the region had been first populated by native Americans, then a scattering of Mexicans, who gave way to immigrants from Texas, Arkansas, and Missouri as the Civil War came on. By the time Stanford reached the area, the sympathizers of Stars and Bars were in the majority.

Stanford laid his tracks in a southeasterly direction, and eventually the line extended south through the town of Tulare, all the way to Bakersfield, one hundred miles from Fresno. By the late 1870s the line had punched all the way through the Tehachapi Mountains into Los Angeles, and a shipping dynasty was born.

The Southern Pacific dominated Fresno, as it did much of the Central Valley; it was Stanford's genius, as well as his fault, to see the great valley as the realm of riches it eventually became, and to desire to rule its affairs completely. A glance at the map of Fresno tells the story: the tracks run southeast, and the streets of the oldest part of the town are canted in a southwest to northeast direction; in order words, to serve the rail line. It was only later, as Fresno began to grow larger than the rail depot that Stanford envisioned, that the streets surrounding the old town were platted on north–south and east–west directions.

Drawn by the fertile soil and the land sales promotions of the railroad, augmented by irrigation ditches and canals, Fresno grew steadily throughout the rest of the nineteenth century. By the early 1920s, the town was a peculiar ethnic mix of Hispanics, blacks, the descendants of the white southern immigrants, and a large influx of Armenians, many of whom came after the massacre in Turkey during World War I.

Then came the Depression, and the Dustbowl years; tens of thousands of small farmers from Oklahoma, Missouri, Arkansas, and Texas, their futures blighted by drought and wind and unforgiving banks and drawn by stories told by their relatives, the descendants of the nineteenth-century southern influx, packed all their belongings into trucks and Model Ts and headed west, just as John Steinbeck recorded in *The Grapes of Wrath*.

And after the Depression came the war, with the high demand for cotton and foodstuffs; Fresno prospered once more, so that by the 1950s, the area around the growing city was a unique mix more akin to what one might find in New Mexico or Texas or Oklahoma than anywhere else in California. The trains rolled in, the trains rolled out; Dwight Eisenhower's interstate highway system improved the long highway known as Ninety-nine, and thousands of new arrivals came to try their hand at working the land, and working those who worked the land—among the latter, a tall, handsome, fiercely ambitious young man named Dale Ewell.

Dale Ewell was a child of the Depression. Born in the fall of 1932, the first of four sons of Ohio farmer Austin Ewell and his Kansas-born wife Mary, Dale was taught from his earliest years to expect nothing but hard work, to regard other men with suspicion; to expect no quarter, and to give none. There was no silver spoon in Dale Ewell's mouth when he was born, in that year of midwestern dust storms, Herbert Hoover, and collapsing farm prices; or for that matter, no bed of roses for his older sister Betty, or his younger twin brothers Richard and Dan, or Ben, the baby of the family.

Austin Ewell worked his two hundred acres in oats, soybeans, corn, and a little wheat, along with cattle, chickens, and hogs. Everyone worked, because, to the Ewell family, that's what life was: work. The way Betty remembered it, years later, the family always had enough to eat; it was money that was scarce.

Some said all the Ewell boys grew up hard-hearted, competitive, and, others said, controlling; it was the way Austin had raised them. Certainly they were all intensely ambitious. And, some whispered, there was no stopping a Ewell, neither law nor morality, when he fixed his eyes on something he wanted, or thought he was entitled to.

Once a man, an acquaintance of Dale Ewell, traveled to Ohio to visit the patriarch, Austin. On the way there, the visitor got lost, and found his way to an American Legion Hall, thinking to quench his thirst with a beer and ask for directions.

"What do you want to see *him* for?" the visitor was asked.

And when the visitor explained his errand, the local pulled a face.

"Old Ewell is a mean, nasty old man who doesn't care about anybody but himself," the local said. "I'll tell you what I mean. I sharpen saws for a living. One day old Ewell come to me with a saw to sharpen. Now, ordinarily my price is seven dollars. But old Ewell says, 'I'll pay you five, and not a penny more.' So I say, all right, and I agree to do her for five.

"Then, wouldn't you know it, the next week, old Ewell shows up again, and he's got a saw with him. He's complaining the work wasn't done right, and now he wants me to do it over, for free! And do you know what? When I looked at that saw, why it was a completely different saw! It was the same kind, all right, but a completely different one. Old Ewell, he wanted me to sharpen that second saw for free, and was trying to trick me into it. All for fiye dollars. Can you imagine that?''

These were the values imparted to his sons by Austin Ewell: abiding respect for the dollar, the appreciation of sweat and hard work, the belief that the other man was not to be trusted any more than the other man should trust you: that is, if he was so stupid you could put one over on him, you should do it. Most of all, though, there was the sense of two worlds—the world of hearth and kin, where one set of values obtained, and the world of the outside, where dogs ate dogs and only fools thought different.

As a youngster growing up on a small farm in northern Ohio, Dale Ewell's earliest years were circumscribed by the rhythms of the soil—planting in the spring, harvesting in the fall, the ingrained knowledge that for everything there is a season, and a natural order. Dale Ewell knew what it was like to get up early, and what it was like to strain his muscles until he was bone-tired, how to sweat until dry. That's the way the world was and the way it always would be, Austin Ewell assured him. But young Dale, when he had the chance, liked to look up from time to time from the endless rows of corn to see the sky; and what he saw there was the beauty and the precision of flight.

By the time he was ten, the world was at war: a global war in which victory would go to the nation with the strongest air power. All over the country, defense plants running round-the-clock turned out engines, fuselages, Plexiglas for windscreens, rivets for airframes, lightweight alloys for hydraulic lines, synthetic rubber for aircraft tires. The skies were filled with flying machines, from the large four-engined bombers to the high-performance fighter aircraft, along with scores of other fabrications—transport aircraft, gliders, observation planes, long-range reconnaissance configurations—each of them more varied, more powerful, more amazing than the last. It was the Golden Age of flight, powered irreducibly by the demands of war. And it was the beginning of a vast industry in which a smart man, if he worked hard, might never have to pick an ear of corn again.

In the fall of 1950, young Dale, then 18 years old, left home for the first time. He enrolled at Miami University of Ohio, in Oxford, where he majored in aeronautical engineering. Dale had his future planned out: first he'd get his engineering degree, his ticket to the glorious age then dawning; then he'd join the United States Air Force and learn how to fly. When that was done, he'd head out to California and go to work in the burgeoning aircraft industry, where jobs were plentiful and the pay was great. After that, who knew? But Dale knew one thing: the airplane business was a long way away from a small Ohio farm; even better, it came with a regular paycheck, and if there was one thing Dale wanted after those Depression years feeding chickens, it was money, and not chicken feed, either.

Graduating on schedule, Dale embarked on phase two of his long-range plan, joining the Air Force in 1954 just after the hostilities ended in Korea. Soon Dale had his wish: the Air Force taught him how to fly. Apparently, Dale was pretty good at it, because the Air Force assigned Dale to pilot a King Air, a twin-engined executive turboprop that then represented the top-of-the-line transportation for Air Force brass. Flying out of Sacramento and later Phoenix, Dale was able to meet many of the Air Force's top generals.

It was in Tucson in 1957 that Dale met a pretty, vivacious University of Arizona student named Glee Ethel Mitchell, the only child of a relatively wealthy Chicago family with roots (and royalties) from the Oklahoma oil fields. Dale and Glee (who had the same first name as her mother, Glee Irvin Mitchell) were a contrasting pair. Where Dale was often taciturn, sometimes even monosyllabic to the point of rudeness, Glee was soft-spoken, open, and socially adept. Some thought Dale was simply shy, acutely aware of the social differences between his rural Ohio roots and Glee's more urbane family. Glee's people had money; Dale's did not.

Glee's mother, Glee Irvin Mitchell, was one of three daughters born to an Oklahoma country doctor, G. E. Irvin. Dr. Irvin was both shrewd and fortunate. It seemed to some that he had a nose for oil. Settling down in Gage, a small town in the western reaches of Oklahoma not far from the Texas border, Dr. Irvin soon began buying real estate and oil leases. By the 1920s, Dr. Irvin was a wealthy man, and by the time of his death, the Irvin family owned land in five different states, including Texas, Missouri, Mississippi, and Arkansas, in addition to Oklahoma. A great many of these parcels held producing oil wells.

When Dr. Irvin died, all three daughters, Glee, Helen, and Grace, managed the real estate and oil properties as a family enterprise, sharing the revenues more or less equally between them.

By that time, Glee Irvin had become Glee Mitchell, married to a man who was an instructor at a Chicago athletic club. When Glee Mitchell gave birth to her own daughter and named her Glee Ethel, the rest of the family began to distinguish mother and daughter by the affectionate nicknames of Big Glee and Little Glee.

Little Glee grew quite close to her Oklahoma relatives, spending each summer in Gage, and once spending an entire year there. A brilliant student, Little Glee's great ambition was to travel the world.

"Her goal in life was to go around the world," her cousin, Jimmie Glee Thurmond, recalled later. "She was the kind of person who wanted to see and do everything."

In 1953, Glee enrolled at the University of Arizona, majoring in Inter-American studies, and took a bachelor's degree in 1957, while winning Phi Beta Kappa honors.

Late that same year, Dale got out of the Air Force, and got a job with Douglas Aircraft in Long Beach, California.

Meanwhile, Glee continued her graduate studies at the University of Arizona.

Whether Dale wanted to marry Glee as soon as she finished her studies isn't clear; what is clear is that Glee had a lifelong interest in travel and meeting people from other cultures, unlike Dale. In any event, in 1959 Glee joined the Central Intelligence Agency.

In later years, this comparatively brief employment with the nation's shadowy foreign intelligence agency—as a translator in Argentina, some said—was seen by some as possibly suggestive of a deeper side to Glee's nature, and possibly as a motive for her murder, however unlikely such a scenario.

After two years in Argentina, Glee resigned and returned to the United States. On December 28, 1961, Dale and Glee were married.

By then Dale had decided that Douglas Aircraft was perhaps a bit too bureaucratic for someone with his ambitions. And Dale had discovered something else, from his years in the Air Force: he enjoyed flying the airplanes more, much more, than he enjoyed engineering them.

In 1959, that in turn led Dale to Fresno, where he soon found a job selling Cessna airplanes—many of them to farmers.

This was something that Dale Ewell was born to do, the perfect amalgamation of his own farming background with his love of flying. Even better, the commissions on the sales of the airplanes were substantial—an order of magnitude above what a salesman might earn for peddling a new car.

Best of all, Dale Ewell knew his customers. Many were variations of his father, Austin. Dale knew how to talk the farm talk, knew the margins of the farm business. He knew about crops and markets and irrigation and water and livestock—hadn't he grown up with his own feet in the dirt?

The Ewell sales approach was unique. Dale wouldn't wait until a customer suddenly decided he or she wanted to own an airplane. If he waited for that to happen, he'd starve to death. No, Dale took the airplane to the customer.

He'd land on a farmer's empty field or an isolated stretch of road, taxi up to an agog farmer's house, and make his pitch: this airplane, Dale would say, was freedom. It was status. It showed the world how successful a man was; literally, the man with a plane had the world looking up at him. Then he'd invite the farmer for a short spin, and the farmer would be hooked.

Just think of it, Dale would say. You buy one of these babies, you can be in Reno in an hour and a half. You can get down to Los Angeles without having to drive for hours and hours. Want to see the city lights in San Francisco? It's just a short hop. And there are ways, he'd add, that a farmer can claim an airplane as a piece of farm equipment on his tax return.

But if a potential customer said he didn't know anything about flying, Dale would say, No problem—I'll teach you myself. And somehow, Dale would have a tractor-bound farmer signing a contract to buy his own airplane, and would sell them flying lessons to boot.

The 1960s were very good years for farmers; an improving economy exploded, and farm prices rose right along with everything else. And, there was an similar explosion of general aviation all over the country, as World War II and Korean veterans grew old enough and prosperous enough to want the romance, and the status, of owning their own airplanes. By the middle 1960s, small aircraft manufacturers like Cessna, Piper, and Beechcraft were swamped with back orders.

The sales commissions on these planes were tremendous. For a top-of-the-line airplane, the commission alone on a single sale could bring the salesman as much as $10,000—flying lessons extra, of course. As the 1960s rolled forward, then, Dale Ewell was beginning to pile up money—a great deal of it.

In 1965, Dale left the Cessna dealership and joined Frank Lambe Aviation, which sold Piper airplanes. Just why Dale made this change is not entirely clear, although some of Dale's acquaintances speculate that Dale wanted larger commissions, and the Cessna dealership wouldn't accommodate him.

Frank Lambe Aviation operated out of a small city-owned airfield just west of Highway 99. Lambe himself was a somewhat controversial figure; police sources in Fresno claim even today that Lambe's full last name is Lambetecchio, and suggest rather darkly that Lambe has in the past had some unsavory associates. In any event, Dale seems to have done much the same for Frank Lambe Aviation as he did for the Cessna dealership: flying Pipers out to isolated farms, and selling the glamour of flight.

By the late sixties, all three of Dale's younger brothers—Dan and Richard, the twins, and Ben, the youngest—had also arrived in Fresno. Dan and Richard went to work servicing agricultural operations, handling the irrigation, the pollination, the harvesting, and packing of the wide variety of crops grown in the valley. Ben attended law school.

All four Ewell brothers soon gained a reputation in Fresno for being hard-driving and competitive. Some thought they were naturally mean, and traced their personalities to their father, Austin. Each of them were sticklers for the printed contract; when a customer, for example, complained to Dale about being overcharged, Dale was contemptuously dismissive. You signed it, Dale would say; you owe it. Don't blame me if you made a bad deal, it's your fault, not mine.

On May 1, 1967, Glee gave birth to a daughter, Tiffany Ann Ewell.

A little less than three years later, on January 28, 1971, Dana James Ewell was born.

2

In the summer of 1971, something unusual happened to Dale Ewell. He was sitting behind his desk at Frank Lambe Aviation when federal drug police came in and took Frank Lambe away.

"If you want anything from your desk," Dale later said he was told, "better get it now, because as of now, this place is closed."

Frank Lambe was on his way to jail, accused of using Frank Lambe Aviation to smuggle in marijuana from Mexico. Suddenly, Dale was out of a job.

Even worse was the prospect that someone, somewhere, might think he'd been involved in Frank Lambe's extra-curricular business affairs. Frank was rough, Dale knew; he'd been on the receiving end of some of Lambe's tirades previously. And another thought: since Dale hadn't been arrested, was it possible Frank Lambe and/or his associates might think that Dale was the one who'd fingered Frank? That was an unpleasant thought.

Dale decided to buy a handgun, just in case. The pistol was a 9-millimeter Browning High-Power semiautomatic. He also bought two boxes of 9-millimeter ammunition. These he placed in the closet of the master bedroom of the house he'd bought for his family on East Park Circle Drive in a fashionably upper-middle-class neighborhood of unincorporated Fresno.

The following year, Frank Lambe was convicted of drug smuggling in federal court and was sentenced to prison. It wasn't long after Frank went away that Dale had a call from the Piper people. Would Dale be interested in taking over Lambe's franchise for Piper Aircraft? The company had a morals clause in its agreement with Lambe, and by being convicted of smuggling, Lambe was in violation of the agreement. The way was clear for Dale to take over.

If anything, this was ideal. Now he was the dealer, not just the salesman. That meant bigger commissions than ever, and in an industry that was even hotter than it had been in the 1960s. Soon Dale moved the business to larger and newer accommodations at Fresno Air Terminal, the jet-capable airport on the city's east side. Leaving Chandler behind was a step up. Dale renamed the business Western Piper Sales. Soon he was outselling anything that Frank Lambe had ever achieved.

In prison, Frank Lambe brooded. Later, he was to tell the *Fresno Bee* newspaper that Dale had reneged on an arrangement Lambe had made with Dale before going to prison. Dale, Lambe said, was only supposed to run the business while he was away. Instead, Dale had taken over the franchise for himself, cutting Lambe out completely. More than twenty years later, Lambe was still bitter, and considered Dale an ungrateful and greedy man.

However he gained control of the Piper franchise, the seventies and eighties were very good years indeed for Dale Ewell. The Piper dealership handled both sales and service, not only for Piper airplanes but others as well. Soon Western Piper's workforce had grown to about a dozen, including sales people and service technicians. The dealership's income was enormous, Dale's chief salesman, Bob Pursell, recalled later—as much as $30,000 in commission was earned on a single sale.

Soon Dale had Pursell doing what he had always done himself—flying the product to the customer. That meant a lot of flying for Pursell, and some dangerous landings in fog and uncertain wind. But Dale pushed Pursell as hard as he pushed himself, with a combination of confrontation, sarcasm, bluster, and guile.

"He was a master at manipulating people," Pursell recalled. "He knew just what buttons to push to get me and everyone else around here to do whatever he wanted. He'd shout at people, or ridicule them. He didn't care how he made people feel. And the thing was, that's what he seemed to enjoy the most—controlling people. It was almost a game with Dale Ewell, to see how far he could go. He seemed to get a big kick out of it—that and putting something over on somebody."

Pursell characterized his relationship with Dale Ewell as a "love-hate" relationship; but others familiar with the ambience at Western Piper during the eighties and early nineties told it differently. They said Pursell only hated Dale Ewell.

The Dale Ewell portrayed by Pursell was a greedy and conniving man.

"His hobby?" Pursell responded when asked. "His hobby was going home to count his money."

Once, Pursell said, he told Dale that he wanted a larger commission on his sales; after all, Pursell said he told Dale, it was he, Pursell, who had to take all the risks landing small airplanes in unlikely places, and in bad weather.

"You'd think he'd be sympathetic to a salesman," Pursell said. "I mean, he'd had to do the same thing himself for years and years for Frank Lambe."

But Dale was contemptuous of Pursell's request. When Pursell suggested that he'd find another dealership where he could make a larger commission, Dale just laughed at him.

" 'You're not going anywhere,' " Pursell said Dale told him.

Later Dale made a counterproposal, Pursell said.

"He told me he was going to make me vice president of Western Piper," Pursell said. "But the deal was, I was going to be an independent contractor. That way I'd get more of the commission."

But what Dale didn't tell him, Pursell said, was that as an independent contractor, his share of the company's retirement program was slashed to a fraction of what it had been before the "promotion." The end result was a net loss for Pursell.

Pursell's view of Dale was of a man so obsessed with money that he was constantly trying to figure out ways to get more of it—even when his net worth was in the multiple millions.

"It was never enough," Pursell recalled. "I once saw bank statements with more than ten million dollars in certificates of deposit. And he still didn't think it was enough!"

More to the point, the Dale described by Pursell was a man who measured a man's worth in the number of dollars he had, in sort of a hierarchical pecking order: no money, no manhood; lots of money, lots of balls. It was as if, Pursell thought, Dale needed money, lots of money, to convince himself—and everyone else—that here was a big man, a man of substance.

Pursell's view of Dale Ewell can be partially explained as the rather jaundiced view of someone who didn't like his boss; but there were many in Fresno who saw Dale in similar terms. By the early nineties, in fact, Dale Ewell had a widespread reputation around Fresno as a grasping, corner-cutting, ethically challenged man who was out for himself, first, foremost, and ever most.

By 1992, Dale Ewell was 59 years old. In addition to the Piper dealership, Dale owned a pistachio farm, a fig ranch, a house on the California coast, a mountain cabin in the Sierra Nevada mountains, a Lincoln Mark VII, a Jeep Wagoneer, and millions of dollars in cash reserves. Indeed, his son Dana, by that year 21 years old, calculated Dale Ewell's net worth at nearly $7.5 million.

But this portrait of Dale Ewell must be incomplete. Because, if Dale Ewell was such a person as described by Pursell and others—mean, grasping, manipulating, belittling—how was it Glee was so opposite? And if he were as others have portrayed him, how could Glee tolerate this behavior?

According to those who knew her well, Glee Ewell was not only a very smart woman—likely, smarter even than Dale—she was also almost universally well liked. For every image of Dale verbally mugging some subordinate, there's another one of Glee: asking after the well-being of friends' children, smiling, being even-tempered, soft-spoken, helpful to everyone.

There's the Glee Ewell who bought bonds to help construct a nonprofit community hospital; or the Glee who donated her time and energy to pass the school bond issues, even though her own children attended private schools; the Glee who supported a multiplicity of civic good works, who served on the county's civil service commission, and the State Board of Bar Governors.

This is the portrait of a giver, not a taker. What would she have made of this man, her husband Dale, who was supposedly viewed with trepidation and suspicion by others?

The chances are, of course, that there were two different Dales. There was the Dale of Western Piper: the aggressive, tough, demanding businessman who gave no quarter nor asked for any. And there was the Dale of East Park Circle Drive, where Dale was far more open, far more loving, than someone like Pursell ever knew.

In all the years he worked for Dale Ewell, Pursell said, Dale invited him to the Ewell house only twice—despite the fact they worked together, and ate lunch together, virtually every working day for nearly twelve years.

Here, then, is an important clue about Dale: like many men who were born in the scarcity of the Great Depression, who came of age in the fifties but before the upheavals of the sixties, Dale's focus was on material success. Money and the getting of money was this generation's war—with the same risks and rewards that earlier and later generations experienced in actual combat. So every deal was a battle, and every battle but another step forward in the unending struggle to win, to conquer, to dominate others before they dominated you.

And when each day's battle was over, the world could be shut out, closed out behind the formidable fortifications of a quiet home life, where the inner circle of family life was lived by altogether different rules.

It was as if Dale Ewell led two lives; in the end, the wall between them was to suddenly crumble, and the cold calculus of the business war/world was to take lodgement in his idealized, cozy world of hearth and home.

3

Some one hundred fifty miles south of Fresno, in the San Fernando Valley of Los Angeles, there is an altogether different world than Fresno. For while the Fresnoans see their city as a small town, no matter its actual size, the residents of the Valley know where they are: they are in a sprawling, mammoth, impersonal megalopolis, mile after mile of asphalt streets, signaled intersections, strip commercial development, separating pockets of tract houses built in the fifties and sixties, cheek by jowl with ticky-tacky apartments thrown up by fast-buck contractors, then pulled down by powerful earthquakes.

In the west end of "the Valley," as Angelenos call it, begins the gentle rise of the West Hills. This is an area of mixed housing, some rich, some poor, but most middle-and upper-middle class, all gently rolling up to the horse country surrounding Chatsworth Peak, the boundary point between the Valley and the run up to the Grapevine.

Sixty years ago this valley was mostly semidesert: dry plains, crisscrossed by seasonal creeks marked by willows and occasional sycamores. The arrival of World War II changed everything in the valley; by the late forties the vast emptiness was almost entirely filled with an enormous grid pattern of streets, twenty-mile-long east–west ribbons like Ventura Boulevard, Victory Boulevard, Sherman Way, and Devonshire, neatly sliced by north–south arteries like Lank-

ershim, Woodman, Reseda Boulevard, and Topanga
Canyon Boulevard, all the way out to Chatsworth and Santa
Susanna Pass. More than two hundred square miles of land
had been transformed into Los Angeles' suburban bed-
rooms.

Many of the new residents came to Los Angeles for the
same reasons that Dale Ewell did in 1957—to work in the
burgeoning aerospace industry. Employers such as Lock-
heed, McDonnell, Douglas, North American, Republic, and
Convair employed thousands of machinists, designers, en-
gineers, and electricians, as tens of thousands of warplanes
and civilian transports rolled off the assembly lines.

One of those who found such a career was Nick P. Radovcich, a brilliant man with a masters' degree in engineering from Massachusetts Institute of Technology, and a
doctorate from the University of California at Los Angeles.
The defense booms of the 1960s and 1980s provided a very
good living for Nick Radovcich and his wife, Judy. By the
late 1970s, Nick and Judy were the parents of seven children, and were living in a comfortable, shady upper-
middle-class enclave in the West Hills, in the farthest
reaches of the valley.

The fifth and fourth Radovcich children were both boys,
Joel, born on August 16, 1980, and Peter, two years older;
both boys attended a nearby parochial prep school, Chaminade. The tuition was steep—nearly $4,800 per child per
year—but the Radovcich family took its religion, Catholi-
cism, very seriously, and the academics available at Chaminade far surpassed those available at public schools.

Despite their closeness, Peter and Joel were a study in
contrasts. Where Peter was clever with his hands and me-
chanically inclined, he seems to have had little interest in
more intellectual pursuits; Joel, on the other hand, was considered by some to be a near-genius, blessed (or cursed)
with a wildly inquiring and doubting turn of mind.

Both boys were handsome, with Joel in particular having
been gifted with dark, luxurious hair and a Byronic sultri-
ness that cast his face with an unpredictable intensity. And

where Peter was content to use his skills in metalworking almost as an artist, to fashion things for the joy and pride of simply being able to do it, Joel had an altogether more creative and imaginative bent.

It was at Chaminade that the two Radovcich brothers met a third valley boy, Jack Ponce. Jack, the son of a prosperous dentist, was thin and restless, but not much of a leader. Jack and Peter became friends in the early 1980s. And while Jack and Peter were close, it was Jack's interest in firearms that captivated young Joel's attention.

In all that was to be written about Joel, Jack, and Peter over the next decade, there is one thing that stands out: theirs was an entirely different sort of generation—not the intense materialism of the men of the fifties, like Dale Ewell, Nick Radovcich, or Jack's dentist father, Dr. Ernest Ponce; nor was it the naive idealism of those who came of age in the 1960s, who spurned personal economic advancement as if it were evidence of a severe character flaw.

The Radovcich brothers and Jack Ponce were of a new generation, children brought into a world of riches, ignorant of the sort of deprivation suffered by Dale Ewell, yet made cynical by the idealistic pretensions of their Baby Boomer older siblings. In another sense, too, the Radovcich brothers and Jack Ponce were war babies: children born during an unpopular war that sapped American belief in institutions and that unleashed the corrosive effect of nihilism, the sense that there is nothing worth believing in: the sad birthright of Generation X.

Later, moralists in the press would wonder just what it was that led such promising futures as those of Joel and Peter Radovcich, and Jack Ponce, into such a grim situation, in which their very lives were at stake, to say nothing of their souls. And it is difficult to isolate anything specific; after all, each of the three had nearly every material advantage life could provide to a young person. Certainly these three were no Dead End kids, surviving the hard knocks of a public housing project, desperate to escape no matter what the cost.

It appears that the road to moral destruction began with nothing more than simple ennui—boredom. Joel, being younger than either Peter or Jack, seems to have been the first to succumb. He began by experimenting with various kinds of destruction.

Joel was different, Peter would try to explain later. He was creative. He'd try different kinds of things just to see what would happen. He liked to shock people, and have people say, That's outrageous, Peter believed. In some way it marked Joel as an individual.

"He would try new things every once in a while," Peter said of Joel. "He would do certain things."

"Certain things like what?" Peter was asked.

"Oh, blow up a CB with one hundred twenty volts instead of twelve."

Likewise, Joel's entire life sometimes seemed to be overcharged. For some reason, Joel's relationship with his father Nick began to deteriorate sharply in the mid-1980s. Later, police and prosecutors would puzzle over this break, knowing only that father and son had little regard for one another, even though no one seemed to be able to pinpoint any specific reason for this.

It does seem clear that one cause of friction between Joel and his father had to do with religion. Joel seems to have repudiated God, or at least the version of God he was taught at Chaminade; for Nick, a staunch Catholic, this was a development that was as unnerving as it was irritating. Whatever the trouble was, it appears to have been considerably exacerbated in the late eighties or early nineties when Dr. Radovcich was transferred to Marietta, Georgia. Rather than move his entire family to Georgia, Dr. Radovcich decided to commute home once a month.

For some reason—perhaps it was after Joel had graduated from Santa Clara University but had no job—when Dr. Radovcich made his monthly commute, Joel would make himself scarce by going to live with friends or his brother Peter. Nick and Joel did not get along.

But in other ways, Joel did not seem to be particularly susceptible to evil, any more than anyone else in his generation. He grew his hair long and wore his grunge clothes the same as other kids of his age, and while Nick sometimes wondered what would become of his fifth child, he hoped and prayed Joel was just passing through a phase.

It was in this experimental phase that Joel decided to attend college. In 1988 he enrolled at his Nick's alma mater, Santa Clara University, a private Catholic university near San Jose in northern California. Nick had graduated from SCU with distinction nearly thirty years earlier.

But getting away from home wasn't the prescription for happiness Joel had thought it might be. For one thing, most of the other students at Santa Clara, Joel believed, were social snobs, more concerned with how they dressed or who they were seen with than anything else. Worse, they looked at Joel as if he were some sort of creep; they thought him unkempt, smelly, and a little squirrelly; and if people said they believed Joel was a genius, it was a pretty fruity genius at that.

Of these three young men, Peter appears to have been the most stable. Forgoing his own chance for college education, Peter had trained to be a jet mechanic; eventually, however, he gave that up to become an on-call plumber in Canoga Park, in the San Fernando Valley. He married a young woman named Danielle. They lived with their dog in an upstairs apartment in Reseda, a few miles away from the plumbing shop. Downstairs in his apartment garage, Peter had rigged up a simple workshop for his welding tools and other equipment. For fun, Peter enjoyed pumping iron.

For his part, Jack Ponce, although he was the oldest of the three, seems to have had real trouble getting motivated in his life. Jack's father, Dr. Ernest Ponce, the dentist, was divorced from Jack's mother. Jack's mother had remarried, and then divorced once more. Jack's home life, then, was somewhat less than stable.

He began attending UCLA in 1986, intending, he believed, to go to medical school. But by the spring of 1991, he still hadn't finished his undergraduate degree, and he didn't seem to be making much progress toward one. His father, Dr. Ernest Ponce, was growing impatient.

Dr. Ponce had been paying his son's educational expenses, and paying the rent on an apartment in Santa Monica near UCLA for Jack. This couldn't go on forever, however pleasant it was for Jack, Dr. Ponce said. The time was coming, he told Jack, when the gravy train would come to the end of the line; Jack had better be ready for it when it happened. Jack shrugged and said he'd try to do better.

The first real trouble began in the spring of 1991, when Joel, living in an expensive Santa Clara University dormitory, Casa Italiana, was caught with two other students in the theft of some of the dormitory's furniture. One of the three apprehended students snitched on the other two, and Joel swore he would get even with him somehow.

Joel was kicked out of the dormitory, and apparently from school entirely for the semester. As a result, he had to return for the fall term at Santa Clara to get his degree.

Nick Radovcich apparently spent much of the summer of 1991 at home, which caused Joel to want to live elsewhere. By the early summer, Joel had worked out an arrangement with Jack Ponce—to live in the Ponce apartment in Santa Monica while Jack took the summer off while living with his mother in San Bernardino.

During this summer, Jack later admitted, he committed a number of vehicle thefts with Joel; according to Jack, he and Joel stole at least two motorcycles and a car, all of which they fixed up and sold for a profit.

But this wasn't all; for some reason, as the summer of 1991 rolled on, Joel began to evidence a peculiar interest in firearms, and, more particularly, in homemade silencers.

Silencers, or sound suppressors, are of course illegal to manufacture and possess in the United States. Certainly Joel knew that, as did, likely, Peter and Jack. Nevertheless,

Joel obtained a variety of paperback books showing the rudiments of making silencers through the use of tin cans filled with sound baffles like tennis balls or steel wool; the use of plastic pipe and duct tape; and most important of all, the use of a drill press to "port," or make little holes in, the barrel of a gun to allow the firing gasses to escape into sound deadeners, thereby helping to muffle the noise of the shot. As the summer unfolded, Joel asked Jack to get him an unregistered gun; and he asked Peter to weld an extension of the barrel of this unregistered gun, an extension that Peter knew was to be used to make an illegal silencer.

That summer, Joel, with Peter's help, made two such silencers, both for pistols provided to him by Jack Ponce: one, a rudimentary affair for a .380 Llama semiautomatic pistol that had been given to Jack by his former stepfather, barely worked. A second, made of a can and tennis balls sliced in half, fitted a .22-caliber Beretta pistol, was marginally better.

Each of the first two silencers was an experiment, it now seems clear, much the same way Dr. Radovcich might check his own engineering sines and cosines. The truly amazing aspect of this summer of experimentation with illegality was that neither Jack nor Peter seemed all that concerned with the import of Joel's behavior; it was as if the moral dimension—the construction of a device to be used to kill another human being silently—completely escaped them. Certainly there seemed to be no qualms or arguments when Joel demanded guns from Jack, or welding expertise from Peter. It was, Peter later tried to explain, just the way Joel was, often doing weird experiments.

But another event at a gun show in Anaheim, California, that summer should have given Jack pause to consider what his friend's younger brother had on his mind.

At the gun show Joel had seen a semiautomatic assault rifle—exactly like the one shown on the cover of one of his silencer books. This weapon was an AT9 Featherlight 9-millimeter rifle—a weapon with a folding stock that could be broken down by unscrewing the barrel from the stock. In short, it was the ideal gun for a silencer, and a silencer just exactly as it appeared in the book he had read. Joel wanted to buy the AT9 on the spot. But when the gun seller wanted to see Joel's identification, Joel refused to provide it. That was when Jack knew, or should have known, that Joel had some very bad ideas of what he wanted to do with this killing instrument.

At the end of the summer, Jack moved back into his Santa Monica apartment, and resumed his desultory progress toward a degree. Joel returned for his final semester at SCU, where his fellow students were surprised to see that one of his closest friends had suddenly become the well-dressed, self-proclaimed multimillionaire student, Dana James Ewell.

4

For the Ewell family, Easter weekend of 1992 was to be spent at Pajaro Dunes, the family's comfortable seaside second home near Watsonville, about ninety minutes south of San Francisco. The holiday was to be the first— and as it turned out, the only—encounter between the Ewell family and the family of John Zent, a Federal Bureau of Investigation agent, whose daughter, Monica, had recently attracted the interest of young Dana Ewell.

The Zents thought the Ewells wanted to look Monica over to see whether she was suitable for their son. Glee and Tiffany had driven down to the beach house on Thursday afternoon; Dale flew from Fresno to the Watsonville airport the following afternoon.

The following evening, Saturday, saw the arrival of Dana and Monica, both students at Santa Clara University, and the Zents, who drove down from their home in Morgan Hill. The dinner seems not to have been a resounding success. The Zents formed the impression that the Ewells were unimpressed by Monica. At one point, Dale told John Zent that Dana wanted to take helicopter lessons that summer. Dale either told Zent the lessons were expensive, or possibly, "too expensive"; it isn't clear whether Dale meant he intended to pay for Dana's chopper instruction even though it was expensive, or if he had refused to pay because it was "too expensive." The subtle difference was to have significance later, however.

After the dinner, the Zent family, with Monica, returned to Morgan Hill. On the drive back, the Zent family discussed their impressions of the Ewells; a consensus was formed that Dale and Glee felt that Monica "wasn't good enough" for Dana.

The next day, the Ewell family departed Pajaro Dunes. Dana left first, driving his 1989 gold Mercedes to Morgan Hill, where he was to join Monica and the Zents for an Easter dinner. Dale left next, driving to the Watsonville airport and the Beechcraft Bonanza airplane he would fly back to Fresno. Glee and Tiffany left last, driving back to Fresno in Glee's 1991 gray Cadillac. Neither Dale nor Glee nor Tiffany had any reason to believe that Easter Sunday, April 19, 1992, was to be the last day of their lives.

5

The killer had the run of the house. He went through all the rooms, exploring, and when he felt like it, pulling out drawers, dumping shelves, and generally making a mess of everything.

In a guest bedroom, he stripped the sheets from the bed, and carried the top sheet into the entry hall bathroom, where he spread it on the floor. As he went through the rooms, selecting items to steal, he returned repeatedly to the bathroom and the sheet; soon the fabric was piled with loot—a stereo, a collection of compact discs, a camera, costume ·jewelry, other odds and ends he found and removed from various rooms.

In Tiffany's room he unplugged a small television set and removed it from its shelf, then put it on the floor as if to say he was undecided about taking it. He opened all of Tiffany's drawers and her closet, and heaped some of Tiffany's clothes in a pile on the floor.

In Glee's small office off the kitchen, he removed his weapon from his backpack and assembled it, screwing the modified barrel into the stock.

In the master bedroom, the killer rumpled the coverings on the ornate double bed, then tore through a closet, removing a .357 Ruger revolver and a shotgun still in its case, along with a leather pouch containing a Browning 9-millimeter semiautomatic pistol and a box of 9-millimeter ammunition. He put the shotgun and the .357 on the bed, but removed the Browning automatic from its pouch, putting it in his backpack. He opened the ammunition box and removed a number of the shells, spilling one on the floor. He loaded his own weapon's magazine with 9-millimeter bullets from the box.

Then he went into the laundry room between the east wing and the family room and waited.

Glee and Tiffany arrived in Fresno from their trip back from Pajaro Dunes around five that afternoon, but not before making a quick stop at a Foster's Freeze so Tiffany could get something cool to drink. Glee drove into the single-car garage on the east side of the house. Then she and Tiffany began to carry things in from the car: an ice cooler, a newspaper, and a few articles of clothing.

They went through the door from the garage into the east wing hallway that went past Dana's room and Glee's office, then turned right past the laundry room and into the kitchen. They put the ice chest down on the round kitchen table, and Glee, car keys still in her hand, turned to go back to the car. Tiffany, carrying a cassette tape, her sweatshirt, and her drink from the Foster's Freeze, turned toward the kitchen table.

The killer stepped unseen out of the laundry room, holding his assault rifle at hip level. He raised the fat black muzzle in Tiffany's direction and fired one shot into the back of her head. The blast thrust Tiffany's body forward, her arms still in front of her; she was dead before she hit the floor, the front of her skull obliterated.

The killer turned immediately and entered the L-shaped corridor leading into the east wing. He saw Glee Ewell stare at him in shock. She ran into the office. He chased her, and fired his second shot, this one striking Glee in the upper-left back and spinning her around as she started to fall. The killer fired again, this time striking her in the upper right arm as she turned. The bullet went through Glee's arm, reentered her body in her right armpit, then cut her spine at chest level before tearing its way through her left collarbone as the blast spun her completely around; she fell on her back, rolled slightly onto her right side. The killer fired a third time as she fell but missed.

Glee lay with her left arm over her face, still alive, stunned and dying. The killer stood over her and fired once more. This time the bullet entered Glee's face and tore through her brain, killing her instantly.

The killer stopped to breathe. He wasn't really sure if the two women were dead. He squatted down near Glee's wrist, and picked it up in his rubber-gloved hand. He felt for a pulse, but detected nothing.

He went into the kitchen, where Tiffany still lay sprawled out facedown on the floor. He squatted down next to Tiffany and tried to detect her pulse, and again felt nothing. He made his way back to the bathroom, and removed his rubber gloves, then put on a new pair. He checked his weapon, and realized the shell catcher he had glued to the breech had cracked. He rattled the casings inside: he hoped there were five. Was that how many times he had shot? The killer wasn't sure.

The killer retraced his steps to the east wing hallway, looking for empty casings in case any had escaped. He didn't find any. He went past the office and Glee's body, and then up the hallway toward Dana's room. He went inside to wait.

Dale Ewell flew his company's Beechcraft Bonanza into Fresno Air Terminal shortly after 4 P.M. After taxiing the aircraft to the company's facility on the west side of the runway, Dale shut the aircraft down and went into his office.

Inside, he found a fax sent to him the previous Friday, after he'd left for Pajaro Dunes. He went through the mail. He called an aircraft engine supplier in Northern California, with whom he was having a feud. After venting his spleen at the engine firm, Dale left the office and climbed into his Lincoln Mark VII to drive home. He arrived shortly after

5 P.M., putting his car into the double-car garage that also held Tiffany's Thunderbird. He crossed into the single-car garage, then opened the door into the east wing hallway. He went down the hallway toward the kitchen; whether he called out to Glee or Tiffany as he came in is known only to his killer.

As Dale made his way down the hallway, the killer stepped out from Dana's room, behind Dale, and fired one last time, this bullet entering the back of Dale Ewell's neck and exiting his throat. Dale went down face forward in the hall, only steps from Glee's office, with the Sunday newspaper, mail, and the late Friday fax falling from his hands as he went down. Like Tiffany, he was dead before he hit the floor. He never knew what happened to his wife and daughter.

6

Tuesday was cleaning day at the Ewell house. This was Rosa Avitia's job, and she'd been doing it for nearly twelve years. With her two assistants, Rosa arrived at the Ewell house shortly before nine in the morning and rang the bell. No one answered.

Mildly surprised to find no one home, Rosa extracted the key the Ewells had given her for such situations, and opened the door. Rosa knew that normally the alarm buzzer would sound softly; she would have forty-five seconds to enter the secret code to keep it from going off full blast. But on this morning the warning buzzer did not sound.

Rosa and her two companions made their way into the entry hall. Almost at once they realized something was wrong: the house was a mess.

"They never keep their home that way," Rosa explained later.

Then, looking into the kitchen, Rosa saw the bloodied remains of Tiffany Ewell, still sprawled on the kitchen floor where the killer had left her two days before. Suppressing her desire to scream, Rosa shoved her companions back toward the front door, where they met a man who was preparing to ring the bell himself.

J. Darwin Knapp had just received a telephone call from Dana Ewell. Dana told Knapp he was worried; he hadn't been able to reach his family by telephone for two days.

Would Knapp check to see if things were all right? Knapp had said he would.

Now Rosa Avitia told Knapp what the three house-cleaners had seen in the kitchen. Knapp went in to look for himself. Yes, it was true: there was Tiffany, clearly dead on the kitchen floor. Knapp and the three housecleaners exited the house once more, and this time Knapp returned to his own house to call the police.

Murder, of course, was hardly unknown in Fresno; for all that civic boosters liked to think of their city as far removed from the corrosive ills of big cities like Los Angeles and San Francisco, the unavoidable fact was that homicide rates had been going up at a frightening rate for more than a decade; and by the early 1990s, as many as 130 murders a year took place somewhere in Fresno County—in actual fact, the highest rate per capita anywhere in the state.

But most of these were predictable urban murders—drunken fights between men over money or women or drugs; husbands killing wives, or wives husbands; or people who killed others in the course of a robbery gone bad. And by far most of the murders took place in the city of Fresno, on the meaner streets where poverty ruled, and drug dealers and prostitutes plied their professions.

The very idea of murder, let alone multiple murder, taking place in the far more genteel precincts of the city's unincorporated southeast section—among the city's rich and powerful—that was very nearly unimaginable to the city's elite. Suddenly, it was as if everyone was vulnerable, not just the poor and criminal classes.

The Sunnyside neighborhood was the bailiwick of the Fresno County Sheriff, an intense, blocky, dark-haired, and well-liked man named Steve Magarian. It was Magarian's Sheriff's Department that maintained order over all of the unincorporated enclaves that had so far maintained their political independence from the city proper, and it was Magarian's men and women who went that Tuesday morning to East Park Circle Drive.

One of the first detectives to arrive at the murder scene was a short, stout, darkly complected, mustachioed man with the unlikely name of John Phillip Souza.

But if Magarian's John Phillip Souza was no bandleader, he would still be the Sheriff's choice to lead the Fresno County Sheriff's Department in what, for the next three years, would be the most frustrating, time-consuming, and expensive investigation the department had ever undertaken.

With Souza that morning were three other detectives: Souza's partner, Ernie Burk, plus Melinda Ybarra and Christian Curtice. Together with their supervisor, Sergeant Dale Caudill, the four would bear the brunt of trying to discover who had so cold-bloodedly killed three-fourths of the Ewell family.

Any homicide investigation begins with a preliminary overview, and this is particularly important in an indoor crime scene such as the one on East Park Circle Drive. This is called the walk-through, as the initially responding police, usually the patrol forces, show the detectives what they have found. It's only after walking through the scene, observing how the victims fell, the probable angles of attack, and locating potential places where evidence technicians might most profitably go to work that detectives can first sit down to theorize about what might have happened.

In the East Park Circle murder scene, Souza and his colleagues rapidly developed two ideas that were later to become critical in the police efforts to solve the case: first, that the two women had been killed first, and by a killer who had waited for Dale Ewell to come later; and second, that despite all the evidence that seemed to suggest that the house had been burglarized, no such thing had actually happened.

In fact, Souza was certain that the putative burglary had been staged in an attempt to throw police off the track.

"It was, probably, the most ransacked residence I've ever been into, burglary-wise, by far," Souza said later. "It was way over—an overkill in searching the residence.''

In vain Souza and Ybarra, along with the rest of the police, searched for evidence of forced entry. There were no pry marks on any of the doors, no broken windows— nothing. And the items piled on the sheets by the putative thief were of no real value. Even the use of sheets instead of pillowcases seemed to show the hand of an amateur, not a real burglar. And when the detectives looked at the open bureaus, they saw another telltale sign: all the drawers had been pulled out from the top down, rather than the bottom up. A professional burglar invariably opens drawers from the bottom up to save time in searching for items of value. And there was the shotgun, still lying in its case on the master bedroom bed. A real burglar would certainly have taken that, along with the .357 pistol, since they could be readily fenced for cash.

No, it seemed certain that the burglary was staged, a cover for the real motive—the cold-blooded murder of three members of the same family.

The detectives now inspected the victims, and here again the killer had left a tale. How was it possible to kill three people all at once, each of them shot from behind? It seemed, from the visible wounds, that Tiffany had been shot first, and that Glee Ewell had tried to escape before being killed herself. And since Glee would have had to go into the hall to get to the garage—after all, her car keys were still in her hand—she would have had to have seen Dale's body if he had been killed first. Therefore, Souza and the others concluded, Dale had to have been killed after Glee and Tiffany.

What did this imply? That the killer, whoever he or she was, had come to the Ewell house for one purpose only—to murder them. All the rest, the evidence of burglary, was a mere blind to throw police off the track.

And finally, what about the alarm? The house was filled with motion detectors in various rooms, including the master bedroom. Yet none of them had sounded. Rosa Avitia swore the alarm was off when she'd entered the house. That had never happened before, she said. That meant the killer either knew enough to disable the alarm, or knew the code to turn it off. That the killer had been in the master bedroom was obvious from the disarray. If the alarm had been on, how was the killer able to get into the master bedroom without setting off the motion detectors?

Detectives searching the closet found a pamphlet describing the gun, a Browning 9-millimeter pistol, and an empty leather pouch for the gun in the nightstand. A box of 9-millimeter bullets was in the nightstand, and a single loose round was on the floor. The gun itself was missing. Talk about leaving a trail: it was almost as if the killer wanted the police to conclude that the Browning had been used to kill the entire family when they surprised him in a burglary. And since it was obvious no burglary had actually taken place, what was the purpose of this charade?

And why? Why did someone hate Dale Ewell so much they were willing to kill his wife and his daughter in the bargain? Clearly, it must have Dale who was the primary target. Otherwise—if the target were Glee or Tiffany—why wouldn't the killer have left immediately after shooting them? Who was Dale Ewell, really? What was the motive for such a seemingly senseless crime—a multiple murder that bore all the contradictory earmarks of both planning and disorganized frenzy?

7

After calling the police, J. Darwin Knapp made a second call, this one to Dana Ewell in Santa Clara.

"You'd better get back here," Knapp told Dana, but he wouldn't say why.

Dana said later that this call from Knapp alarmed him, even more than he'd been worried before he called the family's neighbor.

It's easy to see why: having asked Knapp to check on his family's well-being, to be told cryptically that his presence was immediately required more than one hundred miles away would be disquieting to anyone.

Dana quickly placed a telephone call to John Zent at the FBI's San Jose field office. Dana explained to Zent that he'd been worried about his family, and that he'd had Knapp check up on their well-being. Dana told Zent that Knapp told him to return to Fresno right away. To Zent, that sounded ominous.

Quickly, Zent organized an air trip to Fresno. He picked up his daughter Monica and filled her in. Together they picked up Dana, and all three drove to the San Jose Airport. There they boarded a charter plane and flew immediately to Fresno, but not before Zent called the Fresno authorities to find out what was going on. The Sheriff's Department asked Zent if Dana was returning; when Zent said he was, the department asked Zent to bring Dana to the Sheriff's

Department headquarters as soon as they arrived.

Around noon Dana, John, and Monica Zent arrived at the Fresno Airport. They immediately drove to the Sheriff's Department headquarters on Fresno Street, in the shadow of the peculiar-looking county courthouse, with its thousands of concrete cubbyholes erected to shade the windows that had led its inhabitants to wryly call it the Pigeon Coop. At the Sheriff's headquarters, detectives Souza and Burk waited for their first glimpse of the Ewell family's sole survivor.

What sort of person was this Dana Ewell, they wondered? He would be distraught, they assumed; or, at least, he should be, based upon what they believed he had been told. By that point, Knapp had already told them he'd talked to Dana, and the detectives knew that Zent had discovered that the Ewell family had been murdered. Presumably, the FBI agent had told this to Dana.

Dana James Ewell was 21 years old that spring of 1992. He was tall and lean, with short, neat, slightly curly brown hair. He favored Armani suits, Ralph Lauren shirts, and expensive shoes. He wore business clothes to classes at Santa Clara University, and carried a briefcase with him wherever he went. He endeavored to leave the impression wherever he went that here was a young man on the move, a bold entrepreneur, a precocious multimillionaire intimately familiar with the arcana of high finance and high pressure.

He was not, Souza noticed, very emotional on learning that his father, mother, and sister had all been cold-bloodedly shot to death in their very own house. Instead he seemed more focused on details: what were the detectives doing, what would happen next? He seemed a bit officious, harried, as if the detectives were mere underlings interfering with an important business meeting, a nuisance, necessary perhaps, but still a nuisance.

Souza and Burk watched Dana carefully. Was this the sort of behavior one would expect to see from a grieving

son? Not at all, they concluded almost immediately; and at
almost the same instant, both detectives formed the un-
shakable impression that Dana Ewell was the most likely
suspect in the murders of his own family.

"You always," Souza said later, "look to the family."

And worse, there was Zent. The FBI agent's mere presence at this first meeting with Dana Ewell was an irritant,
almost a roadblock. Zent freely intervened in the conversation, making it clear to the detectives that he, Zent, was
an FBI agent, while they were merely local police officers.

Where was Dana, Sunday afternoon? the detectives
wanted to know. I was with Monica in Morgan Hill, Dana
told them, and later, with John Zent. Both Zents backed
Dana up. When had Dana left Pajaro Dunes?

About two-fifteen or so, he said.

Who left first?

I did, Dana said. Just before my father. He flew back to
Fresno, and my mother and sister drove separately.

How long would it have taken Dale to fly to Fresno from
Watsonville? About an hour to an hour and a half, Dana
told them, including takeoff and landing.

What about the alarm? the detectives wanted to know.
Were Dale and Glee likely to have left it off before going
to Pajaro Dunes?

No, Dana said. Both his parents were "religious" about
setting the alarm whenever they left the house.

Well, did Dana know whether his family had any enemies? No, Dana said, he knew of no enemies of his family.

And now Dana wanted to know something the detectives
thought truly astounding: When would the police be finished at the house? When could he begin making funeral
arrangements?

The detectives told Dana they would have to spend several days processing the crime scene. Perhaps they might
be finished by the end of the week. In the meantime, where
would Dana be staying in case the detectives needed to talk
to him again?

Dana gave the detectives the name and telephone number

of one of his uncles, and said he and the Zents could be reached there. With that the interview was concluded.

The whole encounter set alarm bells clanging in the minds of the detectives. It wasn't just the lack of emotion on Dana's part; there was the matter of Zent. Why had Dana, having been informed by Knapp that there was something wrong at the family house, first called Zent, the FBI agent?

That didn't make any sense—wouldn't it have been more normal for Dana to have called one of his three uncles?

After all, Richard, Dan, and Ben Ewell were in Fresno, and presumably available to go over to the house to find out what was wrong. Why had Dana called the FBI man— unless he was using the FBI man as a shield, and as an alibi?

Dana's odd behavior, when coupled with the failure of the alarm system and the absence of forced entry, along with the obvious staging of the putative burglary, convinced the detectives that Dana Ewell was, for some reason, deeply involved in his family's murder despite his FBI agent alibi. The whole situation reeked of an inside job.

8

Back at East Park Circle, large crowds had gathered outside the Ewell house as the word went through the neighborhood about the murders. Soon Sheriff Magarian himself was on the scene, in the department's mobile command post, a motor home. Police closed East Park Circle Drive on both ends to keep the rubberneckers, who were soon joined by radio, television, and newspaper reporters, out.

While investigators continued combing the Ewell house for evidence—dusting likely surfaces for fingerprints, conducting tape transfers of possible trace evidence from various fabric surfaces, and the like—Magarian met with the newspeople to try to explain what happened.

The situation was shocking to Magarian. He had known both Ewells, Dale only slightly, but Glee quite well, from her service on the Civil Service Commission. To Magarian, Glee was "a neat lady, very kind, very warm and considerate." Magarian thought of Glee as "very sophisticated." To Magarian, Glee had a certain style that clearly identified her as a high-class person, someone cool and perceptive and socially capable. It seemed unfathomable that anyone would want her dead.

Briefly, Magarian explained to the newspeople what the police had discovered inside the house. By then, the neighbors had told reporters of a rash of burglaries that had taken place in the neighborhood over the preceding year. Were the Ewells murdered by the elusive burglar? the newspeople wanted to know.

On this, Magarian had definite information: no. The burglar, he said, had just been caught the week before. On Saturday and Sunday, Magarian said, the very same burglar was being driven through the neighborhood as he confessed to his prior burglaries. There was no way the long-sought Sunnyside break-and-enter man could have been responsible for the murders.

While Magarian was briefing the press, police technicians inside the house were beginning to collect the evidence—most importantly, the bullets fired by the killer. Helping to direct this effort was a twenty-year veteran of the Fresno County Sheriff's Department, Allen Boudreau.

Boudreau was the first forensic scientist ever employed by the Fresno County department. It was Boudreau's job to analyze the evidence to see what it might tell the detectives about the killer, and to preserve its possible usefulness in proving what had happened.

When he arrived at the house early that Tuesday afternoon, it was as apparent to him as the other investigators that the burglary had been staged in an attempt to lead the police astray.

"When I got there," Boudreau said, "one of the detectives, I think it was Mindy Ybarra, took me on a walk-through of the house. And although I haven't been to very many burglaries, within a few minutes of being in there I knew that this was not a burglary. There were just too many things totally wrong."

"This isn't any burglary," Boudreau told Ybarra. "You know, there's quality guns lying here that weren't taken. And look at that"—Boudreau pointed to the stereo component, still on the sheet.

"What burglar do you know who winds up the electrical cord so carefully like that?"

It was true; the "burglar" had carefully coiled the electrical cables for the stereo.

"You're right," said Ybarra, who had, with Souza, already reached the same conclusion.

Boudreau was then briefed by all the detectives, including Souza, Ybarra, and the homicide unit supervisor, Sergeant Caudill. It appeared, Boudreau was told, that the killer's motive was very straightforward. He or she wanted the Ewell family dead.

The bodies of Dale, Glee, and Tiffany still lay where they had been found. One of Boudreau's assistants, Andrea J. Van der Deer de Bondt, took tape transfers from the fabric of the victims' clothing. Later, these tape lifts would be examined for minute particles of trace evidence such as hairs, fibers, gunpowder residue, and the like.

It was readily apparent to everyone that Glee had been attempting to escape when she was killed. She was a particularly gruesome sight lying on her back in her office. It was clear the killer had fired into her face from point-blank range. But when the body was moved, investigators were surprised to find two bullets, one flattened from its impact with the concrete floor, under Glee's body. It was apparent from their weight and size that the bullets were copper-jacketed 9-millimeter rounds, ones very much like those inside the opened ammunition box in the master bedroom.

When he looked at the ammunition box, Boudreau was surprised. There on the outside of the box was a price tag from Sunnyside Hardware, which had gone out of business years earlier. The price for the box of fifty bullets was $7.90.

Gee, Boudreau thought, *based on the price, that's a very old box of ammunition. You can't get 9-millimeter ammunition for anything like that price today.*

Throughout the afternoon, investigators tracked down all the rest of the bullets fired by the killer—one in the kitchen that had exited Tiffany's head and implanted itself in the drywall high up on the wall; one that had struck Dale Ewell in the back of the neck, also found in the wall at the end of the hallway; another in the wall of Glee's office; and a fourth in a flowerbed outside the office, where it had lodged after missing Glee and going through a closet door.

Finding the bullets allowed the investigators to reconstruct with a fair degree of accuracy where the killer had been standing when he or she fired. In addition, Boudreau was particularly interested in examining the murder bullets. One of his specialties was ballistics evidence, and while it was apparent that at least one of the weapons was a 9-millimeter, an initial look at all the spent bullets might reveal whether more than one gun, and hence, more than one killer, was involved.

As the evidence technicians removed the slugs from the walls, Boudreau began his examination. He looked at one of the first bullets to be recovered and started muttering.

"What?" one of the detectives wanted to know. But Boudreau wouldn't say. He wanted to be sure first. He went outside to examine the slug in the sunlight. He put on his glasses.

The bearing surfaces of the bullets—that is, the sides—were marked in a way that bullets weren't normally marked.

Boudreau had viewed literally thousands of bullets in his twenty-year career, but he'd never seen scratches like this before.

"These were very prominent markings," he said.

What could have caused these scratches? Boudreau had an instinct, but he was pretty sure the detectives would think he'd lost his mind.

"I wanted to think about it first. I knew what I wanted to say, but I wanted to think about it," he said later.

These people weren't gangsters, they weren't drug dealers, they are very substantial citizens . . . and this is not Chicago, Boudreau was thinking. *What I'm going to tell these guys will make it sound like the Mafia's been here.*

Boudreau asked the detectives to follow him into the

mobile command post. Caudill, Souza, Burk, Curtice, and Ybarra looked at him expectantly.

"You know," Boudreau told them, "you guys are going to think I'm a crackpot, but these bullets came out of a silencer."

The detectives said nothing at Boudreau's pronouncement. They looked at each other. Boudreau was thinking they were thinking that he'd flipped out.

But nobody doubted Boudreau. In canvassing the neighborhood to see if anyone saw or heard anything—like gunshots—the detectives had come up with almost nothing. How was that possible? The Ewell house was only a few yards away from the neighbors. A 9-millimeter gun going off five or six times was bound to make noise, but no one heard anything—except one neighbor who said he'd heard some unusual noises coming from the Ewell house between 5 and 6 P.M.

Far from thinking Boudreau a crackpot, the detectives were thinking that Boudreau's initial inspection of the bullets had only helped confirm their suspicions.

The killer of the Ewell family had used a silencer; and if nothing else, that surely knocked the aborted burglary theory into the trash can. What sort of random burglar would come into the Ewell house with a prepared silencer for a weapon he or she should have no idea was there?

Yet the idea that the Ewells' killer would have come prepared with a silencer seemed absurd. It was, as Boudreau said, Fresno, not Miami. This wasn't the movies, it was Fresno, for Pete's sake, where the idea of killing someone with a silenced weapon was as foreign and exotic as a magic carpet ride to Timbuktu.

The investigators continued to comb through the Ewell house for the next few days. They learned that a key to the house was normally concealed in a toolshed in the backyard; despite several searches, no one could find it. That opened up a new idea: perhaps the killer had known of the key, and used it to get inside. But how to explain the evasion of the alarm system?

The investigators brought officials from the private alarm company out to the house. The company tested the alarm; it was in perfect working order and, as far as anyone could tell, it had not been tampered with in any way. It was theoretically possible for someone to cut the power to the house, and remove the batteries from the alarm system; but to get there, the intruder would have set off the alarm. There was only one way around this problem, and that was to gain entry through the bathroom skylights. But the skylights were in plain view from the street, and no one had reported seeing any strangers walking around on the Ewell roof on the day of the murders. Besides, it seemed to detectives that the skylights were sealed.

The bodies of the Ewells had been removed from the house for examination and autopsy late Tuesday evening. The autopsy showed what was expected: Dale and Tiffany had been gunned down by a 9-millimeter weapon from behind, while Glee had been shot several times, front and back, as she'd tried to get away. Based on the conditions of the bodies, along with information from Dana and from Dale Ewell's office, it appeared certain that the murders had taken place late Sunday afternoon, probably between 5 and 6 P.M.

A second interview was held with Dana. This time the detectives wanted him to account for his time Sunday afternoon after leaving the Pajaro Dunes house. Again the FBI's Zent was present.

Dana produced a receipt from a Morgan Hill drugstore with the time and the date on it. On the way to see Monica and her family, Dana said, he'd stopped to buy them Easter cards. The receipt proved he was in Morgan Hill Sunday afternoon, as did another receipt from a supermarket where he and Monica had purchased groceries to make the evening meal. He was nowhere near Fresno when the murders took place, said Dana, and the receipts were proof.

Now, suddenly, Dana recalled that his father *did* have enemies.

Who? detectives asked.

Business problems, Dana answered. Maybe Frank Lambe. Maybe Bob Pursell. Maybe drug dealers who were upset with his father for refusing to let his planes be used for smuggling. Maybe the Southern California lawyers who refused to pay the repair fees for the engine work done on their airplane, the same engine that Dale Ewell had been feuding over with the man in Marysville on the afternoon he'd been shot.

Now Dana wanted to know: Was he himself in any danger?

The investigators looked at the proffered receipts. When was the last time *you* saved a receipt for Easter cards from a drugstore, they asked themselves. Agent Zent said the receipts showed Dana was more than a hundred miles away from the scene of the crime, and therefore couldn't have been involved. The investigators thought Zent had been coaching Dana. That was probably why Dana now suddenly remembered that his father had enemies, they thought.

Later the same day, the investigators took Dana on a walk-through of the murder house. Blood still covered the floor in the hallway, office, and kitchen. To the investigators, it seemed that Dana showed no emotion, not even at the sight of the bloodstains. In their view, Dana seemed much more concerned about the condition of the house. He wanted to know if the detectives had taken anything from the residence—as if the detectives were thieves, and were not to be trusted.

The investigators were astonished by Dana's behavior.

Can you believe that guy? they asked each other. And the investigation continued.

9

On the Wednesday evening after the murders, not long after Dana had gone on the walk-through with the detectives, Joel Radovcich suddenly appeared at his brother Peter's apartment in Reseda, in the San Fernando Valley.

Joel was panicked, Peter saw right off. Usually Joel was cool, unflappable, but on this night he seemed wired, nervous, practically paranoid.

"You have to take me out of town," Joel told his brother.

Why? What's wrong? Peter asked.

"Because," Joel said, "I got a code, and I have to get going, get away from here."

Well, Peter said, why don't you just get in your car, then, and drive away? What's stopping you?

Peter didn't understand, Joel told his brother. He couldn't do that. People might be looking for his car.

Looking for Joel's car? Why? Joel's behavior unnerved Peter. Clearly something awful had happened. Whatever it was, Peter didn't want to know what it was. Peter told Joel he couldn't take him anywhere. Joel asked Peter about a backpack he'd left with him a few days before.

Peter found the backpack in the garage, where he'd concealed it a few days earlier at Joel's insistence. He gave the backpack to his brother. Joel took it and left.

*   *   *

On the same night, Jack Ponce was watching television at his girlfriend's apartment in Westwood; his girlfriend was touring in Europe at the time, and Jack had agreed to watch the apartment for her.

The telephone rang. It was Joel Radovcich. He wanted to come over to Jack's girlfriend's apartment, and park his car, a black Honda CRX, in the underground garage.

Jack let Joel into the garage. Joel covered the Honda with a car cover. Jack noticed Joel was unusually nervous.

Joel was saying something about having to leave town right away.

"I don't know what went wrong," he said, again and again.

"What do you mean," Jack said, " 'what went wrong'?"

Joel was shaking, Jack saw.

They got into the elevator to go up to the apartment.

"It has to do," Joel said, "with the triple homicide and me."

Jack shouldn't have had any idea of what Joel was talking about, at least according to his version of the events, since there had been no publicity about the Ewell murders in Los Angeles during the week following the killings; but it didn't take a rocket scientist to know Joel was in some deep trouble.

"Don't tell me anything else," Jack told Joel.

An hour later, Jack went to Peter's apartment in Reseda. They drove to the plumbing shop in Canoga Park where Peter worked. Joel was waiting for them. Joel gave them the backpack he'd reclaimed from Peter earlier in the evening.

"Get rid of this stuff," he told them, and he drove off.

Peter and Jack went into the darkened plumbing shop. They looked in the backpack. One of the first items they discovered was the .380 Llama semiautomatic pistol Jack had given Joel the summer before, the one used in the first attempt at making a silencer. Joel had broken the pistol down into its components. The barrel, with its extension, was just as Peter had welded it the previous year.

Peter smashed the modified barrel across the counter edge, to break the extension off. It went flying across the room, disappearing from view. Peter and Jack spent half an hour searching for it. With the holes ported in the sides of the extension, it was an unusual piece of plumbing equipment, to say the least, and Peter was afraid that if one of his coworkers found it, there might be suspicions. After a frantic search, the extension was finally found. Peter tossed it into the backpack. Then he and Jack left the plumbing shop and got into Peter's truck.

The two friends drove through the night, neither saying much. Every so often, Peter would pull to a stop. Jack would get out, reach into the backpack, and throw something away. Peter drove all the way to Chatsworth Peak, through the Santa Susanna Pass, then back down the mountain into the valley once more. They headed south to Calabasas, then to Topanga Canyon: Books on silencers and weapons went into Dumpsters. Gun parts were tossed into storm drain channels. Tennis shoes went over the side of the cliff in Topanga Canyon; more gun parts into another canyon. Parts of green tennis balls, cut in half, went into another storm drain, along with clumps of steel wool. A paper sack with cartridge cases was ditched in another Dumpster. A length of black PVC pipe was tossed in still another storm drain—eventually, everything in the backpack was scattered to the four corners of the San Fernando Valley.

As they drove, Peter's pager kept going off; it was Danielle, Peter's wife, frantically trying to reach him. After an hour and a half, Peter and Jack finally returned to Reseda and Peter's apartment. Peter ran up the stairs to find out why Danielle had been paging him so urgently. There was just one thing that remained from the backpack. It was a long, black piece of metal. It was the gun barrel of an AT9 Featherlight assault rifle, the very same gun Joel had so coveted the summer before.

Jack decided to dispose of the sleek, black, deadly piece of metal all by himself.

10

On Wednesday, Dana ordered all the locks changed at the Ewell house. He came to the house with one of his uncles, to pick out clothes to be worn by his dead family at their coming funeral service. He was still angry at the detectives, and had lost little of his peremptory attitude. He wanted to know when the police would be finished. Detectives were still evaluating the evidence at the house, they told him. One important piece of evidence was Dana himself, and the detectives observed him carefully.

Dana went into the backyard and approached the toolshed. He reached up to the underside of the roof ledge and removed a key. He put it in his pocket.

Every instinct of the detectives told them to focus on Dana Ewell, his family's sole survivor. "That's the first person you look at," Souza said later.

Apart from Dana's behavior—his seeming lack of grief, his attitude toward the investigators—there was the question of motive: it was obvious that Dale and Glee Ewell were wealthy, and Dana stood to be the only inheritor.

But was this possible? Was it really likely a 21-year-old college student had been able to hire a professional hitman to wipe out his entire family? Leaving aside the issue of Dana's psychological capacity for such a drastic act, where and how could someone like Dana Ewell find a professional assassin? Making contracts with murderers was hardly likely to be part of the curriculum at Santa Clara University's business school.

As the detectives discussed their impressions and their theories, one thing became clear: if Dana was to be the prime suspect, the detectives had better be right. It was bad enough that Dana's entire family had been massacred; to name him as the person responsible would be unspeakably cruel if it wasn't true.

Already, however, speculation was circulating about Dana's potential involvement. The *Fresno Bee* made pointed references to the fact that detectives had interviewed him twice, and to the existence of his alibi; this was sort of a backhanded way of letting the readers know that the detectives had reason to check Dana out. Magarian wanted no slipups on this sensitive issue. Twice in two days he told the *Bee* that Dana was not a suspect, even while seeming to contradict himself by saying the investigation was still wide open, and that no one had been eliminated as a suspect.

The homicide team was under the command of Lieutenant Ron Wiley. Wiley and Sergeant Caudill, the unit's immediate supervisor, sat down to prioritize their investigative tasks. It was clear that the first order of business was to determine the likelihood of the murders having been committed by anyone other than someone connected to Dana Ewell. That meant following up some of the possible leads suggested by Dana—Dale's business problems, if any, or any other possibilities, such as some sort of resentment of Glee, or anger at Tiffany. Only when these possibilities were explored could the detectives be unencumbered in their thinking about Dana.

Detectives Souza, Burk, Ybarra, and Curtice started with Dale's life. Soon a pair of investigators were meeting with Frank Lambe.

It was clear that Lambe and Dale were hardly on the best of terms. Lambe was still bitter over the way Dale had taken over the Piper dealership twenty years before. In addition, Lambe and Dale had sued one another on at least two occasions.

Lambe naturally denied any involvement in the murders. But Dale's death wasn't a complete shock, he said; Dale was a vicious, cutthroat businessman, Lambe told the detectives, and he wouldn't be at all surprised if Dale had stepped on the wrong sort of person.

But in that case, why murder Glee and Tiffany? That was gratuitous. If a business enemy wanted to get rid of Dale, why kill him at home when there would have been ample opportunity at Dale's office, or when he was flying, or driving?

The fact was, Lambe's differences with Dale Ewell went back two decades. It just wasn't very likely that Frank had nursed a murderous grudge for twenty years. If he was going to kill Dale, it would have happened long before. Besides, why kill Glee and Tiffany? What did they ever do to Frank Lambe?

What about Pursell? Detectives had already learned from Marlene Reed, Dale's office manager, that there was perpetual strain in the relationship between Dale and his top salesman. Souza and Burk went to see Pursell.

"Souza looked at me with his cops' eyes," Pursell recalled. "He thought I was the one who did it. He said, 'You had a lot to gain.' Hell, I had shit to gain. He was the one who had the dealership agreement with Piper, not me."

But Souza was only advancing a theory, to see how Pursell would react. After all, if Dale had wrested the dealership from Lambe, who was to say Pursell hadn't tried the same thing with Dale, only this time by murder?

Pursell suggested to the detectives that perhaps the Mafia had rubbed Dale out, maybe to pay him back for some past transgression. Maybe he himself was in danger, Pursell said; who knew whether the mob might think he knew whatever Dale knew?

Souza and Burk questioned Pursell about other possible enemies of Dale. What about this feud over the repaired airplane?

That had been typical of Dale, Pursell told the detectives. Two men had been forced to land at Fresno Air Terminal with engine trouble. They made arrangements for Western Piper to do the repairs, with a new engine to be brought in from the manufacturer in Marysville. For some reason, the repairs weren't done, or done right, but Dale had presented the airplane owners with a bill for $1,700. They refused to pay, and demanded the plane, but Dale refused to release it. He chained the propeller so the aircraft could not be moved. The day before the murders were discovered, the two men had come to Western Piper, cut the chain, and had taken the plane. Marlene Reed had reported the airplane stolen.

Okay, thought the detectives, maybe Dale was less than honest in his business dealings, or perhaps sharp was a better word. But would two men angry over a $1,700 repair bill be likely to kill three people? That was hardly likely. They went to see the two men anyway, and came away convinced of their innocence, along with a further-buttressed impression of Dale as a sharp, sometimes unethical operator.

What about drugs? Had Dale been involved in drug trafficking, as Frank Lambe had been accused of being twenty years earlier?

The aircraft business is particularly susceptible to incursions from the drug trade, in part because of the easy availability of small aircraft for surreptitious smuggling flights.

There had in fact been unsubstantiated rumors that Dale Ewell had some involvement in the drug trafficking business. Five years earlier, he had been called as a witness in a federal drug trafficking case in which a pilot and several other men were accused of using airplanes from Western Piper to smuggle drugs. Among the thirty-four defendants in the smuggling case was a man who had been convicted along with Frank Lambe years earlier.

The allegation was made that Dale had allowed one of his airplanes to be used for smuggling in exchange for money. To conceal the flights, a flight-time measuring device similar to a car's odometer had been tampered with, causing about fifty flight hours to go unregistered. Dale, in his testimony, had been unable to account for the discrepancy. But prosecutors in the smuggling case had ridiculed the missing hours' theory as a diversion, and said there was not a shred of proof that Dale had ever received payment from any of the accused smugglers.

On this point, both Pursell and Lambe were agreed: Dale had no interest in drug smuggling. He was making plenty of money legitimately, they said.

Well, what about Dale's three brothers? Could the murders be the awful result of some sort of previously hidden family feud?

The detectives learned that Dale was not particularly close to Richard, Dan, and Ben, but that was a long way from making the case that the three other Ewell brothers, or any one of them, had anything to do with the murders. Two of the brothers had been involved in a lawsuit over land northeast of Fresno, in which allegations of fraud and bad faith abounded. One of the investors in the Ewell brothers' deal was said to be a Filipino associate of Ferdinand Marcos, and some of the money that had come into the deal was said to be some of Marcos' ill-gotten gains. Could Dale, Glee, and Tiffany have been murdered by a hitman employed by a Marcos associate angry with the other Ewell brothers?

That was even more farfetched, the detectives concluded. Even assuming that a Marcos crony was mad enough to murder, why kill Dale, Glee, and Tiffany—who had nothing to do with the land development deal?

What about Glee's old connection with the CIA?

That idea was patently ridiculous on its face. By all accounts Glee had been a mere translator in Argentina, not some sort of Joan Bond. And, anyway, the employment was more than thirty years in the past. It was hardly likely that some old spy had gone back into the cold to settle the score.

No, just about any way the detectives considered these murders, it all came back to the fact that it was an inside job. Someone had to be able to get into the house without forcing the entry; someone had to know how to turn off or at least disable the alarm system. Someone had to know the Ewells would not be home. Someone had to know they would be arriving separately. Someone had to be familiar with the layout of the house, along with the fact that all three Ewells would enter from the garage area. Someone had to know where that 9-millimeter ammunition could be found. Someone had to be prepared to murder with a silenced gun. And all of these facts were support for the idea that Dana James Ewell knew far more about the deaths of his father, mother, and sister than he was telling.

11

The week following the murders was a confusing one for Joel, Jack, and Peter. All of the events seemed to run together and mix with other, outside events in a sort of surreal pastiche of heart-thumping tension and paranoia.

For one thing, as Jack and Peter made their night ride to dispose of the contents of Joel's backpack, a substantial earthquake struck, rattling most of southern California, and especially Danielle, Peter's wife. That was why she had been so frantically paging Peter throughout the night: she feared her plumber husband had been under a house somewhere when the 6.1 quake hit, and had visions of him lying crushed to death somewhere.

When Peter and Jack reached Peter's Reseda apartment, Jack took the remaining item, the black gun barrel, and walked off. Peter went immediately upstairs to calm Danielle, who wasn't having any of it. Why hadn't Peter responded to the page? Peter didn't want to tell her what he'd been doing with Jack, which made Danielle suspicious that Peter was up to no good.

"I had," he said later, "an extremely angry wife."

For Jack and Joel, the next few hours were very jumbled. Jack later had a difficult time trying to remember exactly what happened, and when it happened. Jack's version of the events went as follows:

After leaving Peter's apartment, Jack went to meet Joel

someplace, although later he could not remember where this was. Joel wanted to hide his Honda. Jack knew of a place in North Hollywood, on a side street. Joel parked his car there, and covered it with a car cover. Then he and Joel drove around.

Joel was still very hyper, continuing to mutter, "What went wrong?" Joel told Jack he'd have to go away to hide out. Joel talked about going to Las Vegas, or possibly Mexico. It seemed to Jack that Joel didn't really want to leave. He didn't want to go to Las Vegas, Joel said, because he didn't know anyone there. Mexico was a bad choice because he didn't speak any Spanish.

"Why don't you get a lawyer?" Jack asked Joel. "I mean, if something bad happened, and you didn't know it was going to happen, it's not your fault."

No, said Joel, he couldn't do that. A lawyer was out. Jack said he then knew for sure that Joel was deeply involved in something very nasty. Worse, now Jack knew the true meaning of some of his own acts over the past year. He was, Jack realized, at least an accessory, if not a co-conspirator. Jack cursed Joel for getting him involved.

"I know, I know," Joel said. "I'm sorry."

Jack edged his way around the topic of what had actually happened. It seemed to him that Joel wanted to tell him everything, but Jack wasn't sure he wanted to hear it. He already knew that whatever the trouble was, it had to do with a triple murder; Joel had already told him that much.

"Well," said Jack, finally, "what's it all about?"

It all had to do with eight million dollars, Joel told Jack. There was another guy involved, and the other guy and Joel were going to split the money.

"We were going to assume the throne," Joel told Jack.

Jack drove Joel back to Jack's girlfriend's apartment. He told Joel that he could stay there for awhile to see how things shook out. When they got to the apartment, Jack noticed for the first time that Joel had shaved all the hair from his body except for his eyebrows.

*   *   *

As the week passed, Joel remained glued to the television set in Jack's girlfriend's apartment. He was particularly interested in watching the news. Yet there was no mention of any triple murder case on Los Angeles–area stations. Bit by bit, according to Jack, Joel let parts of the story emerge. Who was murdered, Jack wanted to know.

A family, Joel answered.

A family was murdered? Why? Why were they murdered?

Jack said Joel told him the other guy, the one who was going to split the eight million with him, was the son of the man who had been murdered. The father, Jack said Joel told him, was being a jerk to his son, and the other guy wanted him dead.

Jack wanted to know if there really was eight million dollars to split.

Yes, Joel said. He'd been shown a financial analysis by the other guy that proved the father's net worth was that much.

What's this other guy like? Jack wanted to know. How can you trust him?

The other guy, Joel said, was very cold, very calculating. He'd even shown Joel how he would cry when he learned that his mother, father, and sister were dead.

Well, what do you think went wrong? Jack asked, certain now that Joel had committed the murders himself.

Joel said he wasn't sure, but was afraid he'd dropped a rubber glove at the scene. He'd wanted to burn the house down to destroy all the evidence, but the other guy didn't want him to do that because there were important papers in the house.

Well, said Jack, what's the other guy's alibi?

The other guy, said Joel, had a great alibi: he was with his girlfriend and her father, who was an FBI agent, when the murders happened.

What's your alibi, then? Jack wanted to know.

I don't have one, Jack said Joel told him.

Jack told Joel that was pretty stupid, and Joel agreed.

Joel said he was going to say he'd been at an all-night auto body shop next to Peter's plumbing shop when the murders occurred. He spent a lot of time there anyway, and no one would be able to say he wasn't there when the killings took place, Joel told Jack.

Two days after the discovery of the murders, a young man named Sean Shelby went to the Ewell house to see what was going on. A longtime friend of Dana Ewell, Shelby soon encountered one of the detectives at the scene. Had the police, he asked, considered the possibility that Dana Ewell was responsible for the murders?

What makes you say that? Shelby was asked.

Because, Shelby said, Dana Ewell was obsessed with money. It was all Dana could talk about. Money, money, money. Dana Ewell was perfectly capable of murdering his family if it meant he'd get to inherit all the dough, the caller said; money was all he cared about.

The detective was noncommittal. It was too soon to know just what was going on, he told Shelby. But the detective took Shelby's name and telephone number, and told him he might be contacted in the future.

Two days later, Saturday, a memorial service for Dale, Glee, and Tiffany was held at the First Congregational Church in Fresno. About four hundred people attended, including a number of detectives.

Dana was accompanied by his uncles, their wives, and their children. They filed into the church and occupied the first five rows.

"What happened in the house?" asked the minister, Rev. Frank Baldwin. "Was it senseless, urban violence or bizarre, twisted killings?" He asked the mourners to pray for the investigators so they might find a solution to the murders.

A number of people presented eulogies for the dead Ewells, including an associate justice of the State Supreme Court, who had known Glee from her stint on the state's Board of Bar Governors.

Glee was lauded as the ultimate giver, and Dale was praised as a strong, determined man. As for Tiffany, the tragedy was even more stark. Only 23 years old, she'd never had a chance to live her life.

Afterward, the surviving Ewells talked with many of the mourners. The detectives watched Dana closely. He still didn't seem to be showing much grief, they thought. Then Dana noticed a recent engagement ring on the finger of a female acquaintance.

"What a rock!" he exclaimed. To the detectives, it seemed that Dale, Glee, and Tiffany hadn't even been buried, yet here was Dana showing more animation over an expensive piece of jewelry than he had anything else up to that point. It was, the detectives told each other, peculiar. Very peculiar.

12

While Sheriff Magarian continued to assure news reporters and the public that the investigation of the Ewell
murders was still ''wide open,'' in actual fact it had
focused on Dana with extreme rapidity. Early the following
week, detectives were already on the campus of Santa Clara
University, seeking to interview Dana's professors and
some of his dormitory mates. Almost immediately they hit
a form of pay dirt.

A professor at Santa Clara told them of an unpleasant
experience he'd had with Dana the previous fall. Dana had
been taking his ethics class, the professor told detectives,
and the professor believed Dana had plagiarized a paper.
When he'd faulted Dana for this, the professor told the
detectives, Dana responded by writing a very nasty letter—
one that appeared, in fact, to be threatening. The detectives
obtained a copy of the letter. They wanted to submit it to
an authority on such communications to see what it might
tell them about Dana's personality.

That Dana was given to grandiosity was also readily apparent. The detectives were shocked to learn that Dana had
been profiled at least five times by various publications,
including, even, the *San Jose Mercury News*. The gist of
the profiles was that Dana James Ewell, a Santa Clara University student, was a self-made, multimillionaire business-
man/entrepreneur.

One such story, in the Santa Clara student paper, seemed to have triggered off the others, including write-ups in *Entrepreneur*, a magazine, and the *Mercury-News*. But reading the *Mercury-News* gave detectives a chill.

". . . marching to a different drummer is something Ewell has always done—and profitably," the newspaper had reported in the fall of 1990.

"At age 19, Ewell is a self-made millionaire who amassed his fortune playing the stock market, running two companies, and selling mutual funds."

Well, this was all clearly untrue. Dana was hardly a self-made millionaire; it was his father, Dale, who was the self-made millionaire.

The story went on to report that Dana "and his investors" had taken over "a bankrupt airplane dealership in Fresno, building it into what Ewell described as 'the Cal Worthington of planes' [Cal Worthington was a ubiquitously televised car dealer at the time] with more than $4 million in sales in 1990, when he sold it."

Dana went on to claim that he kept in frequent contact with business associates on the East Coast. "You never know when an opportunity will present itself," he told the newspaper.

It sounded to detectives as if Dana had taken some of the life story of his father and claimed it as his own. Having falsely claimed Dale's reputation, did that mean Dana might also claim his father's very life? Was that an opportunity that had presented itself?

And what had Dale himself made of his son's braggadocio? Or Glee? After all, the *Mercury-News* was a major newspaper in California. Almost certainly one or more of Glee's many friends in the legal community in San Jose had read of Dana's wild claims and told her about them. It seemed likely they felt that Dana had embarrassed them as well as himself. This could have been cause for friction between Dana and his parents.

What the episode showed more than anything else, though, was that Dana was perfectly capable of lying.

Some of Dana's fellow students described him as fussy
and a bit overbearing. He was very smart, they said—he
claimed to have an IQ of 180. All agreed that Dana was a
very good student. They recalled him particularly because
of his car—a gold 1989 Mercedes—and his expensive taste
in clothes.

Politically, Dana was extremely conservative. He believed that the government was a wasteland of fraud, fiscal
abuse, and incompetence, the last refuge of those who
couldn't make it in the real world. His heroes were Donald
Trump and Michael Milken.

Interestingly, it appeared that Dana had also been fasci-
nated by the so-called Billionaire Boys' Club—a group of
young men in Southern California who had been caught up
in a murder conspiracy involving the manipulation of com-
modity market accounts. Dana was particularly intrigued
with the Billionaire Boys' Club's "paradox philosophy,"
in which good could be made evil and evil good simply by
adjusting one's perspective—the sort of moral relativism
that must have made Dana's ethics professor and the religious authorities at the school throw up their hands in dis-
belief.

Some thought his relationship with Monica Zent was unusual. She just didn't seem Dana Ewell's type, they said.
But that was one of the odd things about Dana. His taste
in friends.

Like, who do you mean? the detectives asked.

Like Joel Radovcich, for one, was the reply. Dana and
Joel were the odd couple. Here was Dana, the multimillionaire businessman/student, with his business clothes and
his briefcase, and his incessant talk about making money,
hanging out with Joel Radovcich.

Who's this Radovcich? the detectives asked.

He's the bad boy of the dorm, came the reply. You
wouldn't think those two had anything in common, but they
hung out together, a lot. Either Joel was in Dana's room,
or Dana was in Joel's room. Dana's room was always spot-
less, Joel's was a pit. Dana wore all those fancy suits, Joel

went around in rags. He was a slob on a skateboard, who didn't bathe particularly often and whose hair was always out of control. Then there was the burglary.

Burglary? What burglary?

Joel had been caught stealing furniture from Casa Italiana, the dorm where both Dana and Joel had rooms. Joel was kicked out of the dorm. The school hadn't prosecuted when the three thieves' parents had paid for the stolen furniture.

This was very interesting information—the fact that Dana seemed to have such an odd acquaintance, and one who had been involved in a crime. The detectives collected a bit more information about Joel, and moved him up on the list of people they intended to interview.

The same day the detectives were finding out about Dana at Santa Clara, the self-same object of the scrutiny met with Detective Ybarra and other investigators at the Pajaro Dunes beach house. The detectives wanted to look over the house for any evidence that might come to bear on the murders.

During a conversation with Ybarra, Dana acknowledged that he'd retrieved a key from the toolshed in the backyard several days before. Why wouldn't he? Dana asked. He'd just changed all the locks on the doors, so the key was useless anyway. What was the big deal?

Well, who else knew this key was available? detectives wanted to know. Dana wasn't sure, but thought probably one or more of his uncles knew where the key was kept. So, too, did the neighbor girl who had the job of taking care of the newspapers delivered when the Ewells were away; she was to put the papers in the toolshed, it appeared.

Had he told anyone else about this key? Dana was asked.

Of course not, he said.

13

The meeting opened at Dan Ewell's office on the next-to-last day of April. Dana was present with his three uncles. Ben, the lawyer, read the last wills of Dale and Glee Ewell.

Dale and Glee Ewell's assets were substantial: nearly three million in cash in various depositories around the central valley. Dale didn't believe much in stocks or bonds; he wanted to have a sizable ready reserve of cash, and he moved this money around frequently to take advantage of various premium interest rates. Some of the accounts were held by Dale as trustee for Dana, while others were held by Glee as trustee for Tiffany; under the terms of the will, much of those funds would be available to Dana immediately, about $450,000.

The rest of the estate—the airplane dealership, the farms, the real estate, and about $1.2 million in a pension plan—would go through probate, and eventually into a trust, the sole beneficiary of which would now be Dana Ewell. The trust was structured in such a way as to avoid giving instant control of all the assets to Dale and Glee's survivors. Instead, the trust would give the survivors control over the principal in stages—income from the principal at 25 years of age, half of the principal at 30 years, and finally, complete control of all the assets at 35 years.

According to his uncles, Dana was thunderstruck. He

leaped to his feet and smashed his fist on the desk.

"Why did my dad do this to me?" he raged.

The day after Dana first learned he would not be able to inherit his father's money all at once, Jack and Joel drove to the beach near Malibu. The day was hot, and as the two sat on the sand, Jack finally decided he had to know what he'd let himself in for.

"Okay," Jack said, "tell me."

Joel was quiet for a bit. Then he said, "I hope there is no God, because if there is, I'm screwed."

He'd murdered three people in a family, Joel told Jack, shooting them just after they'd arrived at their home in Fresno. He reached the house when it was still dark, had parked a few blocks away, and covered the car to conceal it. Then he'd walked to the house—he'd been there once before—and scaled a fence to get into the rear yard. There was no alarm on the windows into the garage, Joel said, and Jack assumed from this that Joel had gotten into the house through one of the garage windows.

Once inside, Joel said, he'd assembled his gun in a room that was an office, and then sat down on plastic sheets he'd brought with him. He'd brought the sheets so he wouldn't leave any hairs or fibers on the floor, Joel told Jack. He'd waited nearly all day.

Joel drew a diagram in the beach sand to show the layout of the house, and what had happened.

The mother and the daughter came in separately, Joel said. He'd shot the daughter first, in the back of the head, just as she'd turned a corner. The mother had her back to him, and she continued talking to the daughter even as Joel was shooting her.

Joel said he'd turned then, and went after the mother. She was facing him when he shot her. He'd had to fire several times. He went back into the office and changed his gloves. He put a fresh clip of ammunition into the gun. Then he sat down to wait for the father to arrive.

A bit later, the father came in through the front door,

Joel told Jack. Joel was hiding when the father came in. He'd shot the father in the front corridor, Joel said.

All three of the people seemed to be dead, but he'd checked their wrists for pulses to be sure. He couldn't detect any, but still wasn't sure the people were really dead. He showed Jack how he'd tried to detect pulses, and Jack told Joel he'd done it the wrong way.

What if he'd somehow failed to kill the people? Was that why he'd gotten the getaway code? Had the people somehow survived their wounds, and were even then describing him to police? But, said Joel, the people he'd shot would have to be great actors to be able to lie still for so long.

Joel told Jack he'd had to wait in the house for several more hours, until it was dark again, before he could leave. He'd taken a 9-millimeter pistol from the house, Joel said, as a "cover weapon," an attempt to lead police to believe that the missing gun was the firearm used in the murders, that, in effect, the killings had taken place during a burglary gone bad. He'd also taken money from the house.

But had he left behind one of the rubber gloves? He wasn't sure.

Jack felt himself sinking deeper and deeper into the morass. He knew now he was as culpable as Joel for what had happened. It was as if they were chained together, and for life. But there was one more thing to find out.

Who was murdered? Jack wanted to know.

"Watch for the name Ewell," Joel told him.

Later that evening, as Jack dropped Joel off at a motel in Santa Monica, the car radio suddenly started going crazy. To Jack, it seemed that the world had gone insane.

Here was Jack, who'd just spent the afternoon sitting on an idyllic beach with a friend, and the friend confessed to murdering three people in cold blood, an act in which Jack was significantly involved, and all of a sudden the car radio was frantic with news bulletins. The verdict on the Rodney King beating trial had come in, and the city of Los Angeles was erupting in riots. Hundreds of buildings were aflame, and scores of people were being shot.

Maybe Joel was right. Maybe there was no God.

Sean Shelby was nervous. The detective kept eyeing him skeptically. But Shelby had made up his mind to tell the police just why he believed that Dana had murdered his own family.

He'd known Dana for a long time, Shelby told the detective, and it was perfectly possible that Dana had set up his parents to be killed. He'd seen Dana at the funeral, and he couldn't believe it, Dana was acting so . . . well, unemotional about the murders.

Later, Sean said, Dana had called him. Dana told him, Sean said, that the police had "bugged" his house. Sean thought Dana's attitude toward this was odd; it was almost as if Dana were boasting about it. Dana told him about his alibi, and the receipts, and it seemed to Sean that Dana was giving him a lecture on how not to run afoul of the police "in case something like this happens to you."

Even weirder, Sean continued, at the end of their conversation, Dana searched him for a hidden microphone.

Tell me some more about Dana, the detective prodded. What was he like, growing up?

He'd known Dana since junior high school, Shelby said. Dana was a spoiled rich kid. Even as far back as junior high school, Dana had loved to flaunt money. Once, when Sean was visiting Dana, Shelby had accidentally tripped over a pile of clothes. A hundred-dollar bill was lying on the floor like so much paper trash. In high school, Dana had once gone to the front of the cafeteria, and in loud, Big Spender fashion, ordered "Hamburgers for everybody!" On another occasion, Dana had hired a limousine to take him to school.

There was more. Shelby told the detectives that as a high school student Dana had paid classmates to perform malicious pranks for him. Once he'd even mused about hiring someone to burglarize his parents' house. It was more than just flaunting of money, or greed for it, that seemed to drive

Dana, Shelby thought. It was as if, in money, Dana had discovered the key to controlling other people—to make them do what he wanted, even if the thing were bad or malicious. He seemed to get off on manipulating people.

But what makes you think Dana is capable of killing his mom, dad, and sister? Shelby was asked.

Because, Shelby said, once in junior high school the teacher asked: Can anyone think of the easiest and fastest way to make money? And Dana said: Kill your parents.

On May 3, the *Bee* profiled Dale Ewell's various business entanglements, seeking to address the question of whether something or someone in Dale's past might have been responsible for the murders.

The *Bee*'s Alex Pulaski searched court records on Dale's business career, and found plenty of fodder. He also talked to a number of people who had done business with Dale, including Frank Lambe.

"Dale Ewell," Lambe told Pulaski, "did not respect you or thank you for anything you had done. My theory, and it's just a theory, is that he stepped on somebody. And he didn't care who he stepped on."

Pulaski reprised the 1987 rumors of the flight-time metering shortages that had resulted in the unsubstantiated allegation that Western Piper was involved in drug smuggling. Now, said Pulaski, Fresno County detectives were looking further into the rumors, even though Lambe, who had gone to prison in 1972 for drug smuggling, said he believed that Dale had nothing to do with smugglers or smuggling.

14

ut if some detectives were poking around in the unsubstantiated reports of Dale's ties to drugs, others were
closing fast on Dana Ewell.

Investigators continued to look for associates of Dana;
by now it was clear that if Dana wasn't available to pull
the trigger himself, but was still somehow involved, the
killer would have to be someone Dana knew. To that end,
the detectives were most interested in Dana's associates,
particularly in the seemingly odd relationship with Joel Radovcich.

Souza and Burk had finally managed to reach Joel on
the telephone. They wanted to set up an appointment to
interview him.

Why? Joel asked.

The detectives told Joel that Dana Ewell's family had
been murdered, and that investigators were trying to talk to
people who had been close to Dana Ewell.

What for? Joel asked.

We're doing a complete background check on the whole
family, the detectives explained.

Joel told Souza and Burk that he'd only known Dana
casually. He was sure he wouldn't be any help to them, he
said.

But when Souza and Burk persisted, saying they really
did need to talk to him, Joel seemed to become alarmed.

"Why?" he asked. "Are you going to arrest me?"

Souza and Burk assured Joel they had no intention of arresting him. Joel finally agreed to be interviewed. He insisted on doing the interview at the motel room the two detectives had booked in the San Fernando Valley. He didn't want the detectives coming to his mother's house in West Hills, he said.

After arranging the interview, Souza and Burk looked at each other. Joel's question about being arrested was weird—unless, of course, Joel had good reason to believe there was a charge on which he might be arrested. The two detectives were now pretty sure they were on to something with Joel Radovcich.

From the beginning of the interview, the following day, Joel seemed to be at pains to explain his "Are you going to arrest me?" question of the day before. Even he seemed to realize it sounded incriminating. But he'd been arrested before, Joel explained, meaning the dorm burglary, and the whole thing about being questioned by police made him nervous, that's all.

Joel said he didn't really know Dana very well. He was just another guy in the dorm, Joel maintained. We didn't have much in common. And I was ahead of him by a few years.

This, of course, wasn't what the detectives had heard on the Santa Clara campus, where they'd been told that Joel and Dana were often in each other's rooms, and were often seen walking together, heads bent in quiet conversation.

Where was Joel on Easter Sunday? the detectives asked.

"Hamrick's," Joel said.

What's that?

An auto body shop, Joel explained.

Anybody see you there?

The owner saw me, Joel said. He remembers I was there that day.

Fine, said the detectives. That's all we need to know right now. But try to keep in touch, we may need to ask you more later.

But the detectives then and there decided that Joel had just made the A-list of possible suspects.

By the middle of May 1992, Richard, Dan, and Ben Ewell and their wives were convinced that Dana was hiding something important about the murders. For one thing, they'd offered a $25,000 reward for information leading to the arrest and conviction of the murderer, and Dana refused to contribute a cent. And when the brothers wanted to put newspaper advertisements in San Francisco and Los Angeles, Dana refused to contribute to this as well.

The three brothers shared their feelings with each other, and began thinking the unthinkable: that their nephew had somehow arranged their brother's murder, along with those of Glee and Tiffany. Then they discussed their feelings with their father, Austin Sr., back on the farm in Ohio. They soon learned that Austin Sr. was also suspicious of Dana.

When the brothers and their father considered it, there had always been something a bit off-center about Dana. There was the arrogance, of course, and the condescension almost everyone felt from Dana, along with his shallow absorption in material things, as if what a person could claim as his was the very definition of his personality. But there was also the hint of a cruel streak in Dana, the sense that here was a rule-breaker, a ne'er-do-well, even, some thought, a sneak and a liar.

Dana just seemed so indifferent to the tragedy. And there was the time when Dan read the wills, only to see Dana explode with rage, and rail at the injustice perpetrated on him by his father. And there were other things, small things, really, but telling in a family: how Dana, in ordering caskets for his father, mother, and sister, had selected the least expensive for Tiffany, remarking, "This one's good enough for her." Or Dana's refusal to pay thirty-five dollars for an extra flower vase in Dale's headstone. Dana said he didn't want to pay the money "Because I'm never going to go there, anyway."

The three brothers compared their experiences with

Dana, who had just moved back into the murder house to live by himself. Finally, it was agreed: the three surviving Ewell brothers would go to the police and share their concerns with the detectives. The investigators were quite interested in everything the Ewell brothers had to say.

It was also in this month, immediately after the murders, that Glee's Oklahoma aunt, Helen Sargent, and her cousin, Jimmie Glee Thurmond, decided to visit Dana's grandmother, Helen's sister, Glee Mitchell.

Mrs. Mitchell, in her nineties, was living in a life-care residential facility some forty miles north of Fresno. Her living expenses were provided for in a life trust that had been administered by her daughter, Glee Ewell. The trust included a number of assets, including cash in various bank accounts, as well as oil rights inherited from her father, Dr. Irvin, in various states. In the aftermath of the murders, Jimmie Glee Thurmond and her mother drove in a motor home out to California. There they spent some time with Dana Ewell.

The Oklahoma family really didn't know Dana all that well, Jimmie Glee was to recall later. Their only contact with Dana was on the occasional trips the Ewell family made to Oklahoma to visit Glee's relatives. To Jimmie Glee and Helen Sargent, Dana was a boy who seemed to have grown up astonishingly fast.

But the Dana they encountered in the month after the murders seemed polite, courteous, and helpful. He escorted Jimmie Glee and Mrs. Sargent to visit Glee Mitchell at the life-care facility, and seemed the very image of a dutiful grandson. Except he could not remain still.

"He was so nervous," Jimmie Glee recalled later. "He sat on the floor of the motor home, moving his feet all around. He could not sit still." Perhaps it was the way young people were, Jimmie Glee and her mother told themselves; but Dana was easily the most excitable person they had met in a long time.

*   *   *

It seemed to Bob Pursell, at Western Piper, that things had spun out of control, like an airplane on its final plunge. However manipulative and cruel Dale might have been to his employees, if there was one thing to be said for him, Pursell thought, it was that Dale ran the place with a steel grip.

Now, with Dale gone, the business was falling apart. All the tensions from the years where Dale had played salesmen against service technicians were coming home to roost with a vengeance, and Western Piper was ripped by intense personal feuds. No one knew what was going to happen.

Into the middle of this maelstrom came Dana. It would be pathetic, Pursell thought, if it wasn't so ludicrous: here was a 21-year-old college student, trying to take over his father's business. And the more Pursell thought about it, the stranger it seemed.

Dana had arrived one morning shortly after the murders, driving his father's Lincoln and even carrying Dale's briefcase. He busied himself patting the employees on the back to encourage them, then went into Dale's office and closed the door. Dana spent literally hours in Dale's office with the door shut, making telephone call after telephone call. No one knew who Dana was talking to. Meanwhile, Western Piper was crashing and burning.

In downtown Fresno, lawyer Michael Dowling looked at what was happening at Western Piper, and also did not like it. It was Dowling who had prepared Dale and Glee's wills, and it was Dowling who was responsible for administering their estate, one important asset of which was Western Piper.

Dowling's role in the affairs of the Ewell family was complex. On the one hand, it was his responsibility to see that the provisions of the two wills were carried out, and the way they were written, that meant as executor he had the obligation to manage Dale's businesses during the probate before liquidation. He had to operate Dale's businesses in a trust for the beneficiary, who was Dana. So that made

Dana a party in interest to Dowling's decisions, along with the estate, even though the estate and Dana might have different, and competing agendas.

In addition to the airplane business, and the fig and pistachio farms, and the beach house, the mountain cabin, and interests in several pieces of Fresno real estate, there were seven bank accounts held by Dale that would be immediately available to Dana—deposits totaling almost $318,000. Another $120,000 would be available from Glee's estate as well, through Tiffany's estate. Dana, as Tiffany's sole survivor, was entitled to that money too.

Finally, because Glee Ewell had been trustee for her aged mother, Glee Mitchell—residing in the life-care facility north of Fresno—that meant Dana had succeeded his mother as trustee for his grandmother. In effect, that gave Dana effective control over Big Glee's money, too—over $380,000 in cash, to say nothing of the income from the oil leases in Oklahoma, Texas, and the other states.

When added together, these various accounts meant Dana could control nearly $800,000 immediately, and much more later, once the estate was liquidated and reinvested. And as the sole survivor of his mother, Dana stood to receive the income from the oil properties when Mrs. Mitchell passed on.

Meanwhile, there were large cash disbursements necessary to keep the airplane dealership and Dale's two farms afloat. Dowling decided he needed to get a court's permission to make those disbursements. While he was at it, he decided, he needed to bring in some professional managers of the farms and Western Piper if the whole edifice wasn't going to collapse. Once things had stabilized, he thought, he could begin the orderly liquidation of the Ewell businesses, and the preparation of the estates' tax returns.

One thing was for sure: Dana wasn't needed to run his father's businesses; he would only be the end repository of the net value, after the expense and taxes—and that, only if he wasn't responsible for Dale, Glee, and Tiffany's deaths.

And here was the most complicated problem of all: the law of the state of California required that anyone found guilty of murder for purposes of collecting an inheritance or insurance proceeds was barred by statute from so collecting. That meant any disbursements to Dana from the estates of Dale, Glee, or Tiffany might eventually be found to be improper. It would be up to Dowling to decide how prudent it would be to provide Dana with money from the estates under the circumstances.

But Dowling wasn't thinking of Dana as a possible suspect in his family's deaths in May of 1992, when some of the Sheriff's detectives came calling. The subject was the two wills, and the provisions in the wills staging the inheritance over fourteen years. Dowling explained how the staging was set up.

How much, the detectives asked, could Dana expect to receive before he was twenty-five?

About $450,000, Dowling said. At that time, Dowling wasn't aware of the cash in the Glee Mitchell living trust, the additional $380,000.

That answered one question for the detectives. Almost a half million now and a lot more later was plenty of motive.

While the detectives did not share their suspicions of Dana with Dowling directly, they did let him know the direction of some of their thinking.

"They made some comment to me, offhand," Dowling recalled later, "something that suggested they knew some things they couldn't tell me right then, but maybe later."

That piqued Dowling's interested.

"Wait a minute," he told the detectives. "What are you guys telling me?" But the detectives only told Dowling they would keep him apprised as their investigation moved forward.

15

It wasn't that the detectives were holding out on Dowling, it was only that they knew they had to go carefully. By now, most were convinced that Dana had arranged the murders. The problem was how to prove it. Dana's alibi was quite clever, and there just didn't seem to be any way to connect him with the shootings.

Sheriff Magarian had been getting some heat over the murders. It was probably the biggest news of the year, and even Magarian knew some would use it as a test for his stewardship of the Sheriff's Department. Were his detectives up to the task? Or were they just incompetent, cow-town cops, as the FBI's Zent seemed to be suggesting?

And when Magarian thought about it—he'd known Glee Ewell personally—he was sure of one thing: if it was within his power to accomplish it, this crime would be solved, no matter how long it took, or how much it cost.

Magarian met with his top brass, and with Lieutenant Wiley.

I want this case solved, Magarian told them. I don't care if you have to put four people on it, full-time. Do it. And so it was that Wiley assigned Detectives Souza, Burk, and Curtice to the case full-time, with Sergeant Dale Caudill in charge as a team leader.

Bit by bit the detectives were starting to assemble portraits of both Dale and Dana. It was striking how similar in some ways father and son were.

Dale was controlling, hard-driven, extremely conscious of money and the making of money; some, like Pursell, considered him a master manipulator. Others, like Lambe, felt he was utterly ruthless.

And here was Dana, said by Sean Shelby and quite a few others, to be similarly manipulative and controlling, and likewise "obsessed" with money. Dana, some felt, was a mini-Dale; and if Dana was behind the murders, if anything that meant he was even more ruthless than his father.

The tales of Dana's past behavior began to form a pattern. Here was a young man consumed with his image. He had to have the best of everything, and was so eager to show off he'd even falsely bragged about his supposed accomplishments in a major newspaper. There had been friction with his parents over that episode; Dana had tried to pass it off as a prank, but Dale was furious and Glee was deeply embarrassed. And there'd been other troubles as well: Dana had been caught perpetrating or organizing several destructive tricks during his junior high and high school years; some thought he had a vicious streak; certainly there were plenty of suggestions of antisocial behavior in his actions.

And there was the letter he'd written to the Santa Clara professor after the accusation of plagiarism in the ethics class. Detectives took this letter to an expert at Fresno State University, who agreed that the letter did seem to hint at a capacity for violence.

In theorizing about the murders, the detectives envisioned a scenario: Dana had decided, for whatever reason, to get rid of his family and take over. It was, after all, a most expeditious way to get rich quick, and without a lot of work, as Dana had supposedly suggested to his junior high school class a few years earlier.

Having made the decision, Dana then set about putting a plan into operation. First, he needed to find someone willing to do the job. It had to be someone susceptible to

Dana's manipulation and control—probably someone just as greedy as Dana. It would be best if the dupe was isolated from his own family, the better for Dana to control him. Dana might offer the dupe a substantial sum of money from the estate, and convince the dupe that Dana was his or her only true friend.

Once the dupe was convinced, the plan would have to call for further careful preparation. The dupe would have to make sure nothing could be traced back, such as a weapon purchase; a date and time would have to be carefully selected to enable the dupe to get into the Ewell house unseen while the Ewells were away; and the murders would have to take place when Dana had activated his own alibi— his date with Monica Zent and the Zent family. John Zent, as an FBI agent, might be manipulated by Dana into intimidating the local investigators, and so was a perfect choice as the alibi.

And in the end, after the heat died down, Dana might act to take care of the dupe, permanently, cutting off the only link with the crime. The dupe would be so trusting of Dana by that point, feeling so conjoined in the conspiracy, he would never suspect that Dana had no intention of allowing him to live.

Of course the plan had huge risks. What if someone saw the dupe going into the Ewell house while they were away? What if someone heard something when the shootings were going on and came to investigate? What if the dupe fired and missed, and one or more of the Ewells escaped to raise the alarm? Even if he or she were successful, what if someone observed the dupe leaving?

But risk-and-reward ratios were part of the lexicon of Dana Ewell's education. Wasn't he the bold entrepreneur, the steely gambler who took plunges and won? Wasn't that how he saw himself?

Hadn't Dana said, "You never know when an opportunity will present itself"?

Had that opportunity presented itself on Easter Sunday 1992?

Where's the weak link in the plan? the detective team asked itself; and the answer was obvious: the dupe.

In considering candidates for the dupe's role, detectives evaluated several possibilities, including a few friends Dana had grown up with in Fresno. But the leading candidate continued to be Joel Radovcich.

Here was someone who seemed to fit the bill: said by fellow students to be a bit off-center, and estranged from others; someone who might be impressed by Dana's putative wealth; someone wild enough to take a crazy risk and break the law, as the dormitory furniture caper suggested. Moreover, after their initial interview with Joel, he seemed to have dropped from sight. Attempts by detectives to re-contact him went unanswered. No one seemed to know where he was.

Then, in one of the occasional slipups that happen in a complex investigation, Joel was finally sighted. The only trouble was, the police officers who saw him didn't know who he was. Joel was, in fact, living at Dana's house.

Having previously decided that Dana was the prime sus-pect, the detectives also decided to keep him under obser-vation. Maybe, just maybe, Dana would make a mistake and lead them to his co-conspirator. Obviously, because Dana had met all the detectives assigned to the Ewell hom-icide team, someone else would have to do the job. The detectives arranged to borrow plainclothes officers from other units of the Sheriff's Department to place Dana under covert surveillance.

Thus, on June 25, 1992, an undercover officer named Toby Rien was following Dana, who was driving his gold Mercedes. There were two people in the car. Rien recog-nized Dana but had no idea who the other person was. Dana and the other man went to a bank. Rien felt that Dana was being careful not to be followed.

The following day, another officer was watching the Ew-ell house when a dark-haired man in a black Honda CRX drove up, activated the garage door opener, and drove in. A few minutes later, Dana himself arrived in the Mercedes. Whoever was driving the Honda, it seemed clear that he had access to the house. The undercover surveillance team watched as Dana and the other man left once more, this time driving to a number of banks.

Just why Joel was not identified at the time of this surveillance is a puzzle. Later, Souza was to say that Joel was not identified as the man accompanying Dana to the banks in late June until the following year, when he showed a photograph of Joel to the undercover officers, who then identified Joel as the person seen driving into the Ewell garage. Just why none of the officers wrote down the license plate number of Joel's car or surreptitiously took his photograph remained unclear.

Since the purpose of the surveillance was to identify Dana's actions and his contacts, this sort of routine investigative effort likely would have confirmed the detectives' suspicions about Joel's relationship with Dana; at the very least it would have answered the question as to Joel's whereabouts.

Whoever the dark-haired man was, it seemed to the surveilling officers that he and Dana were quite close. Both men laughed a lot, and seemed quite happy, the officers reported. It was at this juncture that some detectives began to harbor a suspicion that maybe, just maybe, Dana and his dark-haired friend were lovers.

16

Not knowing Joel's whereabouts prompted Souza and Burk to take another tack. In early July, they decided to make another trip to the San Fernando Valley. This time, they decided, they'd check on Joel's alibi for Easter Sunday, and drop in on his family as well.

The first stop was at Hamrick's, the auto body shop where Joel claimed to be on the afternoon of April 19. The owner of the shop said he didn't remember seeing Joel on Easter. But, said the owner, he suffered from short-term memory problems, and it's possible he did see Joel but just forgot.

I do know one thing, though, said the owner.

What's that? Souza and Burk asked.

I know that Joel told me I saw him on Easter Sunday. That I do remember.

When did he tell you that? the owner was asked. About a month ago, the owner said—just after Souza and Burk had talked to Joel for the first time.

Joel's mother was not particularly helpful to the detectives. She hadn't seen Joel for some weeks. It seemed to her, though, that Joel was acting differently—more standoffish, for one thing, and less communicative. He kept in contact by telephone, but wouldn't say where he was.

Peter Radovcich was a bit more forthcoming. He maintained contact with his brother by dialing Joel's pager when he wanted to talk to him, Peter said.

What's the number? the detectives asked.

Peter said he couldn't remember the digits—just the word it spelled out when it was dialed.

What's that? the detectives wanted to know.

K-I-L-L-A-J-R, Peter told them.

KILLAJR? It hit both detectives at once: Joel Radovcich, killer; KILLA-JR, for Joel Radovcich.

Here was one way to contact Joel, the detectives decided.

But two weeks later, after repeated and unanswered pages from the detectives, Joel canceled the pager account.

By this point, the detectives, still unaware that Joel was living with Dana at the Ewell house, were anxious to talk to Joel once more. They made another trip to the San Fernando Valley, hoping to obtain numbers for Joel's checking account and credit cards.

That way, too, a search warrant for Joel's financial records might show his movements around the time of the killing weekend, as well as his current whereabouts. But the detectives were thwarted. Joel's mother told them that Joel no longer had a checking account, and that he'd apparently stopped using his credit cards.

There was no paper trail for Joel. What was it Dana had told Sean Shelby? Leave a paper trail so you can prove where you were? A Joel without a paper trail was the exact opposite, and this was beginning to appear very suspicious.

Then, in the middle of July, the detectives lost another valuable source—Dana. At the recommendation of Michael Dowling, Dana hired his own civil lawyer, Roger Fipps, and a Fresno criminal lawyer, Richard Berman; he let it be known that he would no longer cooperate with the detectives. Souza, Burk, and Curtice, Dana declared, were incompetent.

"They'll never find out who killed my family," he said.

But Dana underestimated the sheer dogged persistence of the Sheriff's Department, including the efforts of chief criminalist Allen Boudreau.

* * *

Boudreau fully realized that not everyone in the Fresno County department was convinced Boudreau was right about the silencer. It just seemed too exotic.

"You sure?" Boudreau was asked, particularly by department higher-ups who were obviously skeptical of his interpretation of the unusual scratches on the bullets. Boudreau said he was sure, all right. He took a closeup photograph of the odd scratchings on one of the bullets, and mailed copies of the picture to nearly fifty other firearms experts, asking whether any of them had seen such markings before.

Out of the fifty pictures, Boudreau received perhaps six replies; most guessed that the strange scratches were effects left by an exotic weapon, such as a plastic Glock pistol. One investigator in Colorado telephoned Detective Souza to suggest that the marks were the effect of a silencer, but Souza was unable to track the Colorado case down for comparison purposes. Then one day Boudreau took a call from Carlo Rosati, an expert then with the federal Bureau of Alcohol, Tobacco and Firearms.

"Do you have more than one of these?" Rosati asked Boudreau, referring to the marked bullets.

"Yeah," Boudreau said.

"Do they look anything alike?"

"They look like they came out of a Xerox machine," Boudreau told Rosati.

"What do you think about a rusty barrel?" Rosati asked.

"No way," Boudreau said. "You got a rusty barrel, every shot knocks out more rust, they're going to be different."

After a few more questions, Rosati delivered his verdict.

"You've got a silencer there," Rosati told Boudreau.

Boudreau went to see the investigators and told them what Rosati said.

"He thinks it's a silencer too," Boudreau concluded.

Are you sure? Boudreau was asked.

"Yeah, I'm sure," Boudreau insisted. "I'm as sure as I can be without doing any experiments."

Boudreau was getting frustrated. He was convinced that the bullets showed a silencer had been used, only no one seemed to believe him. Now he had one of the leading firearms experts in the nation supporting him, and there were still doubts. But the evidentiary potential of the markings was enormous, Boudreau knew. If ever a suspected murder weapon were recovered, the odd markings would be overwhelming proof, if the markings matched, that the suspect weapon was the one used. The only way to be absolutely sure of the origin of the markings on the murder bullets, Boudreau knew, was to try to find other ways to replicate the markings on a sample 9-millimeter weapon.

Boudreau convinced his superior, Lieutenant Art Cox, to get permission from the Sheriff to start experiments on a seized 9-millimeter pistol. He brought the pistol home and disassembled it, and began making experiments on the barrel in an effort to reproduce the strange markings.

"I tried all kinds of stuff," Boudreau said. "I spent weekend after weekend on my own time trying to figure this out." But the work was frustrating, because no matter what he tried, he couldn't seem to replicate the strange scratches.

By the end of the summer, Boudreau wasn't the only one who was frustrated. Souza and the other detectives kept finding themselves up against blank walls as they tried to look for evidence tying Dana and Joel to the murders.

There was, for example, not a shred of evidence that either Dana or Joel had ever had possession of a 9-millimeter firearm, if you excluded Dale's missing 9-millimeter Browning, which, if one were to believe Boudreau, couldn't possibly have been the murder gun.

Even more frustrating was Dana's refusal to cooperate any further with the investigators. That was a major obstacle, and one exacerbated by intense personal friction between Dana and the detectives. And there was Agent Zent:

the detectives felt hostility from Zent as well, along with what they felt was constant second-guessing by the FBI man. If Dana was behind the murders, putting Zent out front was a master stroke. At the very least, Zent's criticism of the detectives' efforts insulated and seemed to justify Dana's decision to cease cooperation.

Souza and the others plodded along, however, continuing to contact friends and former schoolmates of both Dana and Joel, as well as regularly checking with Joel's mother to see whether he had surfaced. They learned that the last time she'd seen Joel had been in July.

Then the detectives visited the company that had provided Joel's pager account, and obtained a copy of the company's canceled refund check for the deposit on the account. There, on the front of the check, was the answer to Joel's whereabouts: PAY TO THE ORDER OF JOEL RADOV-CICH, 5663 E. PARK CIRCLE DRIVE, FRESNO, CALIFORNIA— the Ewell address.

And on the back of the check were the signatures of both Joel Radovcich and Dana Ewell.

17

With the recovery of the dually endorsed check, detectives for the first time had a positive, documentary link between Dana and Joel, along with a major contradiction in the earlier stories of both. Each had said he was only a casual acquaintance of the other.

Now here was proof that Joel had been using Dana's house at least as a mailing address, if not actually living there. And the double endorsement appeared to answer a second question as well: how Joel had been getting money without using his checking account or his credit cards. Joel, it seemed, was using Dana as a bank.

This documentary information gave the investigators a critical wedge into the hitherto mysterious links between Dana and his former college friend. Investigators prepared an application for a search warrant for the bank and the credit-card records of both Dana and Joel, and for the billing records of telephones associated with both. The various financial accounts were, over the next several years, to provide a wealth of information as to the connection between Dana and Joel, as were the telephone billing records.

While it isn't clear when Dana learned of the police interest in his financial activities, it appears that he must have learned of the probe fairly quickly; because, as the month of October unfolded, Dana's already fractious relationship with the police went into deep freeze.

Late in October, Dana had had enough. His criminal lawyer, Richard Berman, fired off a letter to Sheriff Magarian, complaining of the detectives' actions.

"Dana Ewell adamantly denies any participation in this heinous crime. He had cooperated with you in spite of the fact that he considers your investigation and innuendos to be unprofessional and offensive. If you intend to prosecute Dana Ewell, there are legal procedures. If you intend to just harm him by rumor and innuendo, please be advised that he is prepared to seek every legal remedy for your actions."

Here was a shot across the Sheriff's Department's bow, if there ever was one. Not only was Dana insulting the detectives' competence (some privately cursed the FBI's Zent for giving protective cover for Dana's criticisms), he was actually threatening legal action against the department.

A week later, the dimensions of the confrontation surfaced when the *Bee* published a lengthy article that, for the first time, overtly raised the possibility of Dana's involvement. The newspaper summarized much of the work that had been done by the investigators since the murders, and reported that detectives had talked to many friends and associates of Dana, looking for information about Dana and another student—Joel Radovcich.

This was the first time Joel's name had been mentioned publicly in connection with the murders, and this development seems to have had immediate consequences: Joel moved out of the Ewell house.

The *Bee* also dug up the 1990 *San Jose Mercury-News* story about Dana's claims to be a self-made multimillionaire. The paper went on to report: "Corporate records show that Western Piper was owned by Dale and Glee Ewell and that their children had no ownership stake. Business associates of the Ewell family and family members said Dana Ewell had no significant role in that or any other business. A check of the State Department of Corporations and Fresno County property records showed no company listed under Dana Ewell's name."

The devastating effect of this single paragraph was to show that Dana Ewell had lied in the past; the obvious inference was, perhaps he was lying now.

In a written response to questions propounded by the *Bee*, Dana's lawyer, Berman, attacked the Sheriff's Department for "repeatedly defaming Dana Ewell and his reputation by leaving the impression with his friends, business associates, and in his college community that he is a suspect in this horrible crime.

"Dana feels he is being scapegoated because the investigators have been completely ineffective in finding and prosecuting those responsible," Berman wrote. "If, in fact, the sheriff's office is not intending to spread these rumors, then they should make it clear on the record that Dana is not a suspect."

What had been friction between Dana and the detectives now escalated into open hostility. Stories came back to the investigators that Dana was ridiculing them, referring to Souza and another detective, Curtice, as "Mutt and Jeff," for Souza's short, barrel-chested physique, and Curtice's taller height. They heard that Dana regularly sneered at their competence and intellectual capacities, and made nasty remarks suggesting they were too dumb to do real work, which was why they were employed by the government.

For Souza, an intense individual with stubborn sensitivity, the insults were almost too much. Here was this snotnosed rich kid in the Armani suits, Gucci shoes, driving the gold Mercedes, sneering at him. At him! Okay, so what if he did buy his suits off the rack? So what if he didn't have hundreds of thousands, if not millions, of dollars to play around with, a boat, a private plane, an expensive college education? So what if he lived from paycheck to paycheck, like almost everyone else in the country?

At least he wasn't a triple murderer, Souza thought. And he resolved to prove that that's what Dana Ewell was if it took him the rest of his life.

*   *   *

At the end of November, the pot came to a new boil when the FBI's Zent wrote a long letter to the *Bee*, criticizing both the newspaper and the Sheriff's Department for its treatment of Dana.

After reprising some of the events surrounding his own involvement with the initial stages of the investigation, and contending that Dana had steadfastly endeavored to cooperate with investigators from the beginning, Zent characterized the idea that Dana had hired someone to commit the murders as "grasping at straws." He went on:

"Without question Dana has suffered a great loss compounded by those who would link him to this crime without any factual basis. Eventually someone will be caught who will explain the events surrounding this sad crime, usually after getting off the hook for some other crime."

Zent concluded his letter by avowing his continued support for Dana, and by taking a swipe at the Sheriff's Department.

"The harm," he wrote, "that has been done to [Dana] within Fresno and at Santa Clara University will pass, but none of it has been beneficial to solving this crime. The challenge is to resolve every aspect of the crime, identify the perpetrator, not to simply take aim at Dana in light of one's own limitations or inabilities."

Limitations or inabilities. Zent's letter ignited many in the Sheriff's Department, including Magarian himself.

"John Zent," Magarian offered as his opinion, "is an embarrassment to the FBI."

The *Bee* article about Dana sent Pursell's brain spinning.

Was it possible that Dana Ewell had actually been responsible for murdering Dale?

Pursell thought back to the callow child he had periodically seen at Western Piper.

Dana, Pursell thought, was a "hyper kid." By that, Pursell meant that Dana was speedy, very talkative and energetic. In some sense, Dana was quite different than Dale. He was certainly much more sociable; it was almost as if the Dana Pursell recalled was much more like his mother Glee, animated, socially adept, a live wire.

And the more Pursell thought about Dana, the more he recalled. He remembered hearing stories from his own children, who attended high school with Dana, that the word in the school was, Dana was a big-time coke dealer. In fact, Pursell remembered, at one point he'd communicated these rumors to Dale. Dale had ordered Pursell to shut the door to his office, and had motioned him to a chair.

Dale glared at him.

I never—never—Dale had told Pursell—ever want to hear anything like that from you again. It's none of your business.

Could Dana have been responsible for his family's death? The more Pursell thought about it, the more possible it seemed. Dana, Pursell concluded, was the ultimate proof of the laws of genetics: with his mother's social talent, and his father's driven, compulsive personality, it was almost as if Dana had emerged as the New Model Ewell—the best and the worst of both.

And the more Pursell thought about it, the more it all made sense to him. There was Dana, sweeping into the Western Piper office not long after the murders, playing the role of the Big Boss, toting Dale's briefcase, driving his car, living in Dale's house . . . and now there was the story that Dana had claimed, in the San Jose newspaper, all of Dale's achievements as his own.

It was almost as if, Pursell mused, that Dana had decided to *become* his father. It was, he thought, as if, having lied to the world about his accomplishments, Dana had decided to make them reality by clearing the stage of the unnecessary parents.

Yes, Pursell concluded, it was entirely possible that Dana had murdered his family. What else would you expect? Dale was a man who used everyone, Pursell thought. Now Dale's own flesh and blood had thrown down his trump, and had decided to use Dale—every bit as ruthlessly as anything Dale had ever done himself.

*   *   *

The bank records of Dana and Joel proved very interesting. For one thing, Joel appeared to have no records.

How was that possible? As Souza and the other detectives had learned from Joel's mother, and later, his father, Joel apparently had no job. Nor had either of them given him any money. What was Joel living on—if indeed, he was still alive?

Dana's financial transactions suggested a possible answer. The previous August, Dana had withdrawn $7,500 from his grandmother Glee's trust account. He'd paid his own Visa bill with more of his grandmother's money, and, on September 4, had withdrawn another $1,000 from the same account. Five days later, he went into Glee Mitchell's trust account again, this time for $3,704 for a Visa bill. On the same day, the Mitchell account was used to pay for $1,400 in helicopter lessons—for Joel Radovcich.

This, then, explained what Joel and Dana had been up to during the summer: learning to fly whirlybirds. Souza made inquiries with the helicopter company. He learned that beginning in late June, Dana and Joel had taken a substantial number of flight lessons, paying by cash, personal check, and cashier's check. And, Souza learned, Dale Ewell had been right. The lessons were expensive. On September 5, Joel had received his helicopter pilot's license. To Souza it looked like Dana had paid for this enhancement of Joel's education.

But why? Was this part of a payoff? After all, when the murders had taken place, Dana had expected to inherit Western Piper. Did Joel's helicopter lessons mean that under Dana, Western Piper was going to expand into helicopter services? Were Dana and Joel going to be business partners?

Were they already?

Throughout October and into November, Dana kept raiding his grandmother's account—a $1,000 cashier's check October 6, then a $3,400 withdrawal October 9, two days before Joel paid the flight instructors $1,400 in cash. Later the same month, Joel paid the flight people another $3,400—the same amount taken by Dana from his grandmother's account on October 9.

To Souza, these large withdrawals seemed to show two things: one, that Dana was financing Joel; and two, that Dana, as the successor trustee to his mother for his grandmother Glee, was busily looting his aged grandmother's estate.

In November, after the *Bee* article recounting Dana's possible viability as a suspect, and mentioning Joel's name for the first time, Joel contacted the flight instructors and directed them to refund any unused portion of his flight lessons to . . . Dana Ewell.

On November 10, 1992, Dana was called into the Sheriff's Department offices in downtown Fresno for the ostensible purpose of returning to him Dale's .357 Ruger revolver. When detectives tried to ask him questions about Joel, Dana refused to discuss the matter. It seemed to the detectives that Dana was practically running as he left the Sheriff's Department offices.

The following month, Dana paid another Visa bill with his grandmother's money—this time, $7,900.

Where was all this money going to? While there didn't seem to be any way to prove it—at least not yet—the detectives' hunch was that somehow, through some means investigators had not yet discovered, at least some of this cash was getting to Joel Radovcich.

THE MIDDLE GAME

18

On February 1, 1993, a rolling surveillance team of fourteen undercover Fresno Sheriff's deputies set up shop on Joel Radovcich not far from his mother's house in West Hills. The intention: to watch what Joel did, to see how he came by his money, and to document any further contacts between Joel and Dana Ewell.

Rolling surveillance is a peculiarly difficult task, especially when the surveillor doesn't want the surveillee to know what's happening. The major difficulty is that the surveillance subject knows where he is going, but his shadows don't.

To cover the available possibilities, a large team may be required, along with effective communications. And, if the surveillance is to last a long time, a truly effective rolling surveillance requires that the covert observers be changed on a daily, even hourly, basis. This can cut down on the quality of the surveillance product; naturally, a constant rotation of observers diminishes the ability of the observing side to make sense of what they are seeing, because they are deprived of the continuing context; some officers, for example, might not know the significance of an action that would have made complete sense to someone watching two days before.

Such surveillance, of course, is also enormously expensive. But, given the seeming inability to break through

Dana's denials, a crack at Dana's supposed dupe was thought to be worthwhile. Perhaps Joel wouldn't be as clever as Dana; and if Joel were indeed the killer, perhaps he'd make some mistake that would lead investigators to hard evidence—like the gun.

The Fresno County Sheriff's Department was hardly awash in excess personnel; like most other police agencies, there was always more than enough to do with the available person power, let alone running off to the San Fernando Valley, more than a hundred and fifty miles away, to conduct comprehensive observation on Joel Radovcich.

But Magarian gave the operation his approval. Hadn't he promised to bring the Ewells' killer to justice, no matter what? Money wasn't an issue, Magarian made clear, not if it meant a chance to solve the case.

So, on February 1, 1993, rolling teams of narcotics officers and other detectives began tracking Joel Radovcich's movements. On the first day, the team followed Joel from his mother's house in the San Fernando Valley to a bank of pay telephones in Canoga Park. Later the same evening, Joel drove south to El Segundo, where he stopped at a gas station and made more pay telephone calls. After hanging up, Joel continued south to Seal Beach, where he stopped at a convenience store to make still more calls. At that point, the surveillance team decided to see if one of the undercover officers could get close enough to Joel to hear what he was saying on the telephone.

A detective named Pursell stood at an adjacent phone and pretended to make his own call, while striving to surreptitiously eavesdrop on Joel.

"Come on down," Pursell later said he heard Joel say. "You ought to be down here . . . I don't know, a helicopter." Pursell heard Joel give some details of weather conditions over the Grapevine, the highway over the mountain passes north of Los Angeles. Then Joel said something that electrified Pursell.

"Both your parents and your sister," Pursell said he

heard Joel say. "Give me the keys and we'll have a party at the house."

Both your parents and your sister? A party at the house? Was Joel referring to the murders? Was he talking to Dana? Joel seemed flip, almost irreverent. Talk about your cold-blooded murderers; these guys were something else, Pursell thought.

Much later, this overheard snatch of conversation was to be quite controversial. While Detective Souza assumed that the conversation was with Dana Ewell, the evidence is rather more murky. A later check with the telephone company for records of calls made from the telephone used by Joel showed no record of any long-distance calls at the time Joel was using the telephone. Was the conversation entirely innocent, as lawyers for Dana and Joel later insisted? Was it with Dana, or someone else—perhaps with one of Joel's girlfriends, whose parents lived in Seal Beach? Still, for the detectives, the possibility that Joel was chiding Dana about the murders was tantalizing. Later, the conversation would be used by Detective Souza as evidence in his efforts to get arrest warrants for Dana, Joel, and Jack.

After hanging up once more, the surveillance team followed Joel to an apartment in Huntington Beach, where it appeared that he was living.

In the days following, the rolling surveillance tracked Joel to various locations in Southern California, including Long Beach Municipal Airport. There, it was learned, Joel was taking still more flying lessons—and still paying in cash.

While the surveillance teams kept watch on Joel, the homicide detectives continued trying to develop leads on Joel and Dana. Souza, for example, learned that after Joel had graduated from Santa Clara University in December 1991, he continued to frequent the Santa Clara area, seeing friends and acquaintances there. Now several of these acquaintances told Souza that Joel had boasted to them that he would be a millionaire by the time he was twenty-five.

One, in fact, claimed to Souza that Joel had bragged that he had "a cop-proof plan."

All of this was additional grist for the suspicion mill, but still woefully short of evidence. Then, on February 3, Detective Ernie Burk uncovered the thread that was to lead to potentially productive results, indeed.

Tom Duong was also a Santa Clara University student, as had been his brother, Tony. Now Burk learned that for a time in the spring of 1991, Joel Radovcich had stayed at the Duong brothers' parents' house. Joel had asked Duong if it was all right if some magazines he wanted to order by mail were sent to the Duong residence and received in Tom's name. Duong agreed to this. Under no circumstances, Joel told Tom, should he open this package.

The day came when the package arrived. Either Tom forgot Joel's instructions not to open the package, or he was simply curious; in any event, Tom *did* open the package. The very first book turned out to be an instruction manual: "How to Make Silencers." Altogether there were ten different books, all from the same publisher, and covering such things as silencers, explosives, booby traps, wiretapping, and similar black arts.

Duong was at first shocked, then angry at Joel. He knew that it was a federal offense to manufacture noise suppressors for a firearm, as it is to wiretap. And booby traps! What if someone found out that he, Tom Duong, was ordering these kinds of books? Tom told Joel what he thought of him for using Tom that way, and Joel apologized, saying it wouldn't happen again.

Who published these books? Burk asked Tom Duong. Can you remember?

Tom thought for awhile. It was, he said finally, something like Presidio Press . . . or maybe not that exactly, but something like it. But this reminded him of something else, Tom told Burk. Back in 1991, Joel had asked if Tom could get him a gun somewhere.

When I asked him why he just didn't go to a sporting

goods store and buy one, he wouldn't say, Tom told Burk. But now that I recall this, I also remember he was mad at somebody who'd been in the dorm furniture caper with him, and who'd snitched Joel out . . . Joel had said he intended to get even with the rat . . . maybe that's why he wanted a gun, and a book on how to make a silencer. Maybe he intended to get even with this other guy.

Maybe, said Burk. But Burk had a pretty good idea of how any silencer that may have been made by Joel might have been used.

Now the investigators decided to turn up the heat a little. It seemed to them that Joel was the weaker of the two possible conspirators; and if Joel thought the police were closing in on him, he might panic.

But how could they communicate this to Joel? Such a proactive strategy had possibilities, but only if Joel could receive the message. How could this be done? The story in the *Fresno Bee* the previous fall had seemed to have some effect on Joel; after all, when that article named Joel as a person police were interested in, Joel had moved out of Dana's house. Maybe the same thing would work to trigger a new reaction in Joel.

On March 23, the *Los Angeles Times* ran a page 3 story about the Ewell murders, written by Mark Arax, himself a native of Fresno. Joel was included in the detectives' discussion of the case.

Essentially, the *Times* article was a rehash of the information reported the previous fall in the *Bee*. But there was one new thing added:

Joel, Arax reported, had "dropped out of sight after being questioned.

"Investigators," Arax added, "said they are trying to find Radovcich to question him again."

Well, this wasn't quite accurate, since the detectives had been shadowing Joel for the better part of two months, and they had a pretty good idea of exactly where he was. But letting Joel—and his family—know that he was wanted for new questioning might well precipitate incautious movement by Joel. And that movement might lead investigators still closer to Dana.

To the surveilling detectives, Joel seemed despondent. They tracked him to UCLA, and later Malibu. Three days later, the investigators cranked the heat up another notch by making arrangements to search a trash Dumpster that had been used by the Radovcich family. In the trash detectives found a freehand sketch. The sketch showed a human head exploding.

After watching Joel for two months, the surveillance teams had learned a few things about Joel: first, he liked to drive fast. Second, he was very partial to pay telephones, including one at a convenience store about a mile away from his mother's house in the San Fernando Valley. The third thing was that Joel had another pager—replacing the one he'd canceled the summer before, the KILLAJR number.

On April 1, 1993, the day after detectives searched the Radovcich Dumpster, Joel drove from his mother's house to the pay telephone at the convenience store, located at the intersection of Saticoy and Fallbrook in West Hills. As Joel began dialing, one of the undercover officers, a Sergeant Hollis, noted the time, stood at the pay telephone in the adjacent booth, dropped in a quarter, and pretended to make his own telephone call, while straining to eavesdrop on Joel's end of the conversation, just as Pursell had two months earlier.

Later a considerable controversy would ensue over these overheard conversations. Was this a form of illegal bugging? Some said it was, no different than any other unwarranted invasion of privacy, such as unapproved wiretapping or placing an illegal microphone in a briefcase or under a table.

Others, however, contended that it was no different than overhearing a loud conversation in any other public place, such as a bar or restaurant. Since the booth being used by Joel was a public telephone booth, open to the surroundings, he was not entitled to an expectation of privacy.

Even more controversial was the supposed content of the conversation—or at least, the part attributed to Joel. Sergeant Hollis readily admitted that he could only hear bits and pieces of the conversation; that he wasn't taking notes or otherwise trying to record the portions he overheard; and further, that it was noisy outside, with all the traffic going by, and so it was quite likely that he hadn't heard everything.

In any event, Joel dialed a long-distance number from the telephone at Fallbrook and Saticoy while Sergeant Hollis strained to hear what Joel was saying and to whom he was talking. The call lasted for nearly thirty-one minutes. Under the conditions, Sergeant Hollis was later to say he only overheard the barest snatches of Joel's side of the conversation.

Just the same, Hollis said he overheard Joel make the following statements:

"I'm at Mom's house."

"Need to find a place."

"I don't want to stay long."

"They might drive by and see me."

"Got a lawyer."

"Can't do buddy-buddy system."

"Have you had any heat yet?"

"Twenty-five thousand big ones for doing nothing."

"I didn't tell them anything."

As anyone can see, either this is hardly a complete list of everything Joel said during this call, or the other party to the conversation was doing most of the talking, since, added together, these phrases would account for less than two minutes of the thirty-one-minute telephone call.

Even Hollis was later to admit that he was basing his repetition of things he believed he'd heard Joel say on his memory only, and that it was entirely possible that other things had been said that either Hollis didn't hear or couldn't remember.

After the conversation was over, Joel hung up and drove

away in his black Honda, while Hollis tried to recall everything he'd overheard.

Just after 5 P.M., Joel returned to the same pay telephone. This time, another detective, Jimmy Lee, took up the adjacent position.

Joel dialed a number, and then hung up almost immediately. He waited for nine minutes, then received a signal on his pager. He dialed once more. This conversation lasted a little over twelve minutes.

Detective Lee later said he overheard Joel make these statements:

"I wanted it taken care of before this."

"There's going to be a news blitz."

"I think this thing is going to blow up."

"We're going to have to do something before the news—"

"I don't want no fucking stock options."

"One quarter million and I want it now."

"I want to go around the world."

According to Lee's surveillance report, on the following day Detective Lee was again at the convenience store when Joel arrived once more. Joel made another two-second call, then hung up. A few minutes later, Joel made another call, this time engaging in conversation. This time, Lee said, he overheard Joel make these statements:

"I have a feeling this thing is going to blow up."

"What about that."

"I need money."

As with the fragments Hollis claimed to have overheard, both of these conversations were likewise the subject of intense controversy; it didn't help matters much when Detective Lee later admitted that this might not have been exactly, word for word, what he'd overheard, or even the actual days that he'd heard it. Matters were worsened when Detective Souza used the bits of overheard conversation to get his arrest warrants, and had Lee overhearing Joel use the name "Dana" during the conversation. Lee, however, later denied that he'd heard Joel say the name "Dana."

Still, taken altogether, these supposed statements by Joel on April 1 and 2, 1992, might possibly be inculpatory; after all, Joel seemed to be asking for money, "no fucking stock options"; and he seemed to be indicating a desire to get out of town, as well as fear that "the thing" was ready to "blow up."

But the conditions of the eavesdropping, along with the accuracy (or lack of it) of Detective Lee's memory, made reliance on the statements risky. Most of all, at that point detectives had no way of proving who it was Joel had been talking to.

Consequently, the detectives obtained a search warrant for the calling records of the pay telephone used by Joel. The first call, the thirty-one-minute conversation April 1 overheard by Sergeant Hollis, went to a pay telephone at a gas station in Santa Clara approximately four minutes by car from Dana Ewell's dormitory, the Casa Italiana; the afternoon's two-second call witnessed by Detective Lee was to a number registered to Dana Ewell's dorm room; and the third call of the day was to the first location, the Santa Clara gas station.

The April 2 calls went, first to the dorm room number; and second, to a Wendy's restaurant in Santa Clara not far from the Santa Clara University campus. Later the detectives were to learn that this fast-food outlet was often frequented by Dana James Ewell.

19

To the detectives, it appeared that the proactive strategy was having some effect on Joel. In the week following the surveillance at the Saticoy and Fallbrook pay telephone, Joel drove to Fresno. By this time, as the detectives knew, Dana had returned as a full-time student to Santa Clara University. It appeared to the surveillance team that Joel had unfettered access to the Ewell house in Dana's absence. Joel was also tracked to the offices of a Fresno criminal lawyer, Terrence Woolf, a former deputy district attorney.

Two days later, the *Fresno Bee* published a one-year-after story on the murders. After recounting the details of the killings and the swirl of rumors that had surrounded them, the *Bee* said it appeared that the detectives had focused on Dana, and on Joel.

"They spent considerable time searching for a college classmate, Joel Radovcich," the *Bee* reported. The *Bee* said it had been suggested in news reports—a reference to the *Times* article a few weeks before—that detectives were having trouble locating Joel, an implication that Joel was hiding.

At that point, Joel's recently hired lawyer, Woolf, surfaced publicly for the first time, to defend Joel.

"He doesn't want to be in the public light," Woolf told the *Bee*, "but he has not been hiding. Detectives talked to him and he gave them a full and complete statement. He is not a suspect.''

Further, said Woolf, if detectives were having a hard time finding Joel, it was only because they hadn't looked hard enough.

For his part, Dana issued a written statement that blamed the news media for worsening a tragic situation.

''On April 19, 1992, four wonderful lives ended in tragedy,'' Dana said in his statement. ''My father, my mother, and my sister were brutally murdered. My world was shattered, and my life was changed forever. The reality of a loss like this can hardly be imagined even after this length of time.

''I must say,'' the statement continued, ''this tragedy has been deepened by those in the media who have spread gossip and innuendo, which was unsupported by fact or distorted reality. Those reporters who have been inaccurate or sensationalist in their stories are doing a disservice to the public, my family, and me.''

The very next day, the surveillance team followed Joel to Santa Clara. After another series of pay telephone calls, Joel was seen getting into Dana's gold Mercedes. They drove to the San Jose airport, and stayed together until about 6:30 P.M.

Meanwhile, Joel's use of a pager at the Saticoy and Fallbrook convenience store telephone had reinvigorated the investigators' interest in Joel's use of the pager system of communication.

Depending on the system used, the device could pass on messages, telephone numbers, or simple notification that a message had been received. What sort of system was Joel using? Even more interesting, who had Joel been calling, or—who had called Joel?

By the first week of April, the detectives had written a search warrant for records associated with Joel's pager. But this was to be a different sort of warrant, one almost akin to a wiretap. Because, in addition to the records of calls incoming and outgoing, the investigators wanted to get an exact duplicate of Joel's pager.

That way, it was calculated, any call made to Joel could be received by the detectives, too.

On April 12, while Joel was on his way to Santa Clara, Souza personally delivered the approved search warrant to a business in Beverly Hills, California, where Joel had previously established his new pager account. The company executives read the warrant and assured Souza that such a thing was technically feasible.

But something went wrong. For one thing, the duplicate pager didn't seem to work properly; also, because of tests conducted by the detectives and the pager company, Joel soon realized that someone else was using his device.

Nine days after getting the duplicate, Souza returned to the Beverly Hills company and complained that the duplicate pager wasn't working properly. The company officials reprogrammed the device. Two hours later, Joel also arrived at the pager company, demanding to know whether anyone had served a search warrant in connection with his pager, or his call records. The company denied this.

Joel wanted to know whether anyone else could have the same number that he had, and the company officials denied this as well. They told Joel that possibly his pager number had been hijacked by dope dealers; and that maybe the drug dealers were responsible for the strange numbers he had been seeing on his pager.

Joel wasn't satisfied with their explanation, company officials told Souza the following day. Joel demanded that his name be removed from their computer, and reregistered at a new number as "Mike Smith." The officials assured Joel this would solve the problem. The day after that, the company again reprogrammed Souza's copy of Joel's pager, so Souza could keep track of who Joel was calling, and who was calling him. Over the next few months, this capability, when joined with the telephone records of pay and private telephones used by Joel and Dana, resulted in a variety of new leads.

One of those leads, in fact, was eventually to lead detectives to Joel's old friend Jack Ponce.

It had been almost exactly a year since Jack and Peter Radovcich had thrown away the materials contained in the backpack Joel had given them.

It hadn't been an easy year for Jack. As promised, his father had cut Jack off from further financial support when he'd failed to graduate from UCLA by the end of 1991; 1992 had been a horrible year, even forgetting the nightmare of April, when he and Peter had thrown out what they both believed was incriminating evidence against Joel, and the week afterward, when Joel had told Jack most of the gory details.

Jack continued to plod through UCLA for the rest of 1992; he finally graduated in December of that year with a degree in history—a bit short of the premedical school education that Jack had once hoped to obtain.

He'd seen Joel on several occasions throughout the year, and on a couple of occasions Joel had given him some money. Jack moved in with his mother in San Bernardino, and finally was able to get a job—as a bartender at a restaurant in Ontario, California, TGIFriday's. It was, all things considered, not exactly what a graduate of UCLA might have expected.

Just when Jack was beginning to hope that the ugly Ewell mess would fade away, the article in the *Los Angeles Times* jolted him back to reality. Both he and Peter, Jack realized, were at the very least accessories after the fact, if Joel had actually committed murder; Jack wondered whether they might also be considered co-conspirators for what they had done.

Peter had also read the March 22, 1993, *L.A. Times* article, and immediately called Jack to discuss it with him—especially the part referring to Joel. Did it mean that the police would be after them too? Then had come the detectives' search of the Radovcich family trash, which the family had soon learned about; it seemed to Jack that the detectives had clearly focused their attention on Joel as the prime suspect in the murders.

When Jack thought about it, he realized that he'd taken one small step after another, all the way down the primrose path; now, he knew, he was in so deep that they only way out was to keep his mouth shut, now and forever, unless he wanted to go down for the count too, along with Joel and Dana Ewell, whoever he was.

Jack didn't like it, but there wasn't anything he could do about it. He was roped to Joel Radovcich for better or worse.

20

By late April, Joel had moved again, this time to Costa Mesa, also in Orange County. He began new flying lessons, again paying cash, with his old flight instructor at Long Beach Airport. Over the next week Joel paid a little over $1,000 for these lessons. Still he had no job.

Having turned the heat up on Joel with the Dumpster search, the detectives were ready to activate part two of their plan to destabilize their quarry. This time, they intended to use Dana himself as the trigger.

On May 12, 1993, Detectives Chris Curtice and Ernie Burk went to Santa Clara University. They made sure Dana saw them in the morning as they waited outside one of his classes. They followed him back to Casa Italiana. Dana immediately telephoned the Santa Clara Police Department to complain that two men were following him.

Later, the two detectives shadowed Dana to the campus bookstore, where Dana confronted them. Dana asked them, somewhat sarcastically, whether they were enjoying their visit to the university.

That night, around 8 P.M., the detectives decided to pull the trigger. Accompanied by two campus security officers, the two detectives visited Dana in his dormitory room.

"What are you doing here?" an angry Dana demanded. Behind Dana the two detectives could see that Dana had a visitor, Monica Zent.

We want to talk to you, Curtice told Dana. We know who killed your family.

To Curtice, it seemed like Dana wasn't interested in hearing this.

"This isn't the right time or place," Dana told Curtice. He began berating the campus police for allowing the two detectives into the dormitory. The detectives should call him later, Dana told them, after he'd talked to his lawyer, Richard Berman.

"That's okay, Dana," Curtice said. "You know how to get ahold of us, and we know how to get ahold of you."

That, of course, was a not-too-subtle suggestion that Dana himself remained a suspect in the murders, and that the detectives could "get ahold" of him whenever they wanted.

Dana began to close the door, when Curtice pulled his Columbo act.

"By the way, Dana," Curtice said, "we think Joel Radovcich killed your family."

Dana, said Curtice, had a visible reaction to this statement.

"He looked like he'd been punched in the gut," Curtice said later. "He just basically looked at me, said 'Okay,' and then shut the door."

Now Curtice and Burk settled down to wait.

Within a few minutes, both Dana and Monica left the dorm. First they went to the campus security office to complain about the two detectives being allowed into the dorm. Then they went to the student parking lot and got into Dana's Mercedes. Curtice and Burk followed them to see what they would do. Dana pulled onto a nearby freeway, drove a few miles, then suddenly cut across three lanes of traffic as if to ditch the pursuing Curtice and Burk. The detectives weren't able to get over in time to exit themselves. Dana had given them the slip.

Fifteen minutes after Curtice and Burk lost surveillance on Dana and Monica, Souza's duplicate pager went off. Someone was calling Joel Radovcich. Joel was asked to call a telephone number in Santa Clara. Now the detectives were ready for the second act. Souza was parked near Joel's Costa Mesa apartment, waiting to see how Joel might react to Curtice's gambit.

At almost the same time, Curtice and Burk telephoned Souza on a cellular telephone to let him know they'd lost sight of Dana and Monica. Frantically, Souza searched his list of known pay telephone numbers in the Santa Clara area so he could tell the Santa Clara team where Dana might have gone. The number flashed to Joel's pager wasn't on the list.

Another detective called the telephone company to ask for the address of the unlisted Santa Clara pay telephone, which turned out to be in an office complex not far from the campus. The detectives raced to the location. As they entered the parking lot they saw Dana's Mercedes just pulling out.

What did all this mean?

While it was far short of proof that Dana and Joel had conspired to murder Dana's family, at the very least it suggested that Dana was hardly interested in assisting the detectives in their investigation into the murders of his father, mother, and sister.

It appeared, in fact, that Dana was doing everything he could to thwart them, up to and including possibly providing a warning to Joel that police might soon arrest him. This was not, the detectives decided, the sort of behavior one might expect from an innocent person.

This psychological goosing of Dana wasn't the department's only proactive attempt to destablize Joel. The following day, Curtice and Burk contacted a former Santa Clara University student named Jennifer Nunnikoven. The detectives had been told that, apart from Dana, Jennifer was one of the few in the Santa Clara set who was close to Joel.

It appeared to detectives that Jennifer was more than just a friend to Joel Radovcich. But both detectives thought Jennifer tried to minimize her relationship with Joel, and Curtice and Burk believed she was being evasive.

Both detectives, however, thought it likely that Jennifer would soon call Joel to let him know that the detectives had been to see her.

The following day, the twin surveillance efforts paid off in another seeming contact between Joel and Dana. It appeared to the investigators that Joel and Dana were exchanging information about one topic, and that topic was Jennifer Nunnikoven.

Dana had flown into Fresno Air Terminal in his twin-engined Piper that afternoon. A surveillance team saw him at the airport at about 5:30 P.M. Around that same time, Souza's duplicate pager went off, and Joel was directed to call a pay telephone at the Airport Holiday Inn in Fresno, across the street from the place where Dana kept his plane.

Just before six that afternoon the team on Joel saw Joel go to a pay phone in Costa Mesa. Again the eavesdropping technique was employed. This time, the surveilling officer reported overhearing the following conversation by Joel:

"I'm getting a little worried."

"Play it cool, don't worry about it, she doesn't know anything."

"She's about ready to burst."

"Can't say anything, she won't."

"I miss you."

"They think they've got something, you know, evidence."

"They need to make an arrest, politically, they need it."

"Just play the game, I think it's going well."

"I advise you not to talk to them."

"We have nothing to gain and everything to lose."

"They are going to lock you up."

"I can't be around you, my life is fucked."

"You need to keep on repeating it, they will play on your fear."

"I love you too."

"Don't talk to them."

"You don't have to talk, just don't say anything."

"They don't have a gun to your head."

"They can't tap your phone, it's against the law in this country."

"If you love me, you won't say anything."

"They spread lies."

"They have to trip you up."

"They try to catch you in a lie."

"If you talk to them they'll mix you up and twist your words."

Later, the investigators were to contend that this entire conversation was conducted between Joel and Dana; they pointed to the supposed statements by Joel "missing" Dana, and "I love you" as a possible indication that Joel and Dana had a homosexual relationship, a claim that was later vehemently rejected by their lawyers.

But since the conversation seemed to have had to do with a third-person conversation about Jennifer's dealings with the detectives—"she"—and the remainder appears to be more intimate, the possibility exists that the surveillance team on Joel had mashed together *two* conversations—the first with Dana Ewell, the second with Jennifer herself, and perhaps as many as two other conversations, with still other people.

Later, lawyers for Joel and Dana were to point to this eavesdropping sample as an example of how the Fresno County Sheriff's Department detectives had developed that bane of homicide investigators, the so-called tunnel vision.

Having been told by the homicide detectives that their quarries were Dana and Joel, the surveillance officers heard statements made by Joel and attempted to twist them to fit their understanding of what was happening, or so the defense lawyers contended.

In their attempts to defend Joel and Dana, the lawyers contended that the surveillance teams had hopelessly commingled the various statements they said they had overheard. Not only were the recapitulations from memory faulty, Dana and Joel's lawyers asserted, the police were totally and irretrievably mistaken as to who was talking to whom. Indeed, many of the eavesdropped-upon conversations were between people other than Dana and Joel, they contended.

The May 14, 1993, conversation stood as Exhibit A in this argument.

The first three or possibly four phrases attributed to Joel could be interpreted as conversation between Joel and Dana—if, indeed, Dana was still in the area of the airport at approximately 6 P.M. Because there apparently was no close surveillance on Dana at the time Joel was at the pay telephone in Costa Mesa, there's no way of knowing whether *any* of the overheard statements were made to Dana.

By referring three times to "she," it seems that Joel might have been referring to Jennifer, and commenting on the fact that detectives had visited her the previous day.

"Play it cool," Joel was alleged to have said, "she doesn't know anything." This is part and parcel of the same reassurance, and communication: "She's about ready to burst," and "Can't say anything, she won't."

It wasn't very likely that this conversation was with Jennifer, not with the subject identified as the third-party "she."

If Dana was at the other end of the phone, the phrase "I miss you" might have been uttered to either Dana or Jennifer herself; but the rest of the eavesdropped content is open to a different interpretation.

In fact, it is possible that portions of the remaining conversation may have been uttered by Joel to Jennifer herself, in order to assuage her concerns about the visitation by police.

Telling Jennifer that the detectives "needed to make an arrest, politically, they need it," could well be seen as an attempt by Joel to explain to Jennifer what was going on. Certainly, Joel, if he was a co-conspirator with Dana, would not have needed to tell his fellow plotter not to talk to detectives; in any event, Dana had already refused to talk any more with the investigators.

Most of the remainder of the supposed conversation could be interpreted as applying more to Joel's relationship with Jennifer than Dana. Again, the repeated advice, "Don't talk to them," supplemented by "I can't be around you, my life is fucked," to say nothing of the importunings to say nothing further.

Still, the surveillance reports on Joel for this particular day say nothing about his making *two* telephone calls; and when summarizing their evidence nearly two years later, the detectives asserted that they believed "the [entire] preceding conversation developed as a result of the contact with Dana and detectives in Dana's dormitory room."

In other words, the detectives believed that Joel's overheard conversations on May 14, 1993, two days after investigators tried to trigger Joel into a panic reaction to the assertions made by detectives to Dana, were evidence of guilt by both Dana and Joel.

Four days later after this May 14 conversation, the detectives revisited Jennifer; they asked Jennifer to take a lie detector test, and she agreed. But on the same day, the surveillance team assigned to Joel watched him go to a pay telephone in Costa Mesa. It seemed to the officers that Joel had telephoned Jennifer.

The one-sided conversation, as overheard, seemed to indicate that Jennifer told Joel that she intended to take the lie detector test. The report of Joel's words:

"Oh my God, oh my God, Jen."

"Jennifer, did you talk with your parents about this?"

"Oh, Jen, lie detector tests are very false, all right."

"Oh Jen, Jen, you're getting yourself in way too deep."

"Oh, don't trust them, no."

"Jen, Jen, Jen, why?"

"You're only gonna get yourself in deeper, all right."

"I bet you, a bogus test, because, Jen, not just a ruse, hopefully you dump information that you don't know."

"Jen, don't interpret that."

"Jen, you need a lawyer."

"Jen, you're in too deep."

Following this conversation, Joel was overheard calling Fresno information for Woolf's number. Having reached

Woolf's office, Joel was said by the surveilling undercover officer to have told Woolf that a friend of his had been asked by the Fresno Sheriff's Department to take a lie detector test. Subsequently, Joel made another telephone call, and asked someone to call Woolf.

The overheard conversation, as reported by the surveillance officer:

"Yeah, Jen, this is serious shit, you could get yourself in way too deep, quick."

"Ha-ha, they know I have an advantage, okay, I already answered them. All that stuff was bullshit."

"I advise you not to take it until you get counsel."

"Jen, it's not that simple. You're going to get ramrod[ded] by the Sheriff's. . . ."

"Oh my God, oh my God, you're over your head and you'll be going, oh my God, you know, you're just over, you're just going to be so over your head and you're going to destroy your life out of this."

"They will destroy your life."

"Just call my guy. And I advise you to seek his advice."

What did any of this stuff mean?

To anyone with tunnel vision, it seemed clear: the conspirators, Dana and Joel, were communicating; more, they were attempting to plug any possible leaks, by dissuading Jennifer Nunnikoven not to take a lie detector test.

But was that the only way of interpreting the one-sided conversations—even assuming the eavesdropping was accurate?

Seen from another perspective, Joel's allegedly overheard remarks could be interpreted altogether differently.

Far short of indicating responsibility for the murders, these conversations could easily be explained as nothing more than the natural reaction of a person (or persons) to having been targeted as a suspect in a horrible crime. The police were trying to implicate them; it was only reasonable for those who had come into the ambit of police interest to discuss that fact with one another, and to commiserate.

The Ewell house, in a well-to-do neighborhood in southeast Fresno. More than four years after the murders, the house remained unsold. *(Photo by Carlton Smith)*

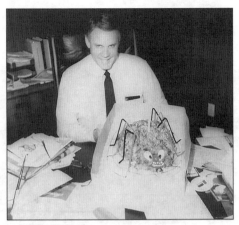

Dale Ewell, at his desk at Western Piper, on his birthday several years before the murders. The senior Ewell was widely regarded throughout Fresno as a hard-driving, even ruthless, businessman. *(Photo by Bob Pursell)*

Glee Ewell, wife of Dale and mother of Tiffany and Dana, was a high official in the California State Bar. She and Dale seemed to pursue largely separate public lives. Here she receives a Bar award for work benefitting legal assistance for the indigent from Fresno County Municipal Court Judge Robert Oliver, and former State Bar President Don Fischbach; California State Senator Ken Maddy is lower right. *(Photo by Howard Watkins)*

Casa Italiana, the exclusive University of Santa Clara dormitory, where Dana Ewell met Joel Radovcich. Police contended that the plot to kill Dana Ewell's family was hatched here in the winter of 1991-92. *(Photo by Carlton Smith)*

A bank of pay telephones near the University of Santa Clara. Police traced critical calls made by Joel Radovcich to the center telephone, and believed that Dana Ewell was the recipient. *(Photo by Carlton Smith)*

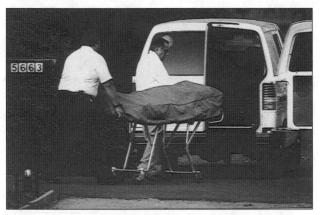

Fresno County officials remove the body of one of the Ewell victims, April 21, 1992. *(Photo by Kurt Hegre, reprinted by permission of the* Fresno Bee*)*

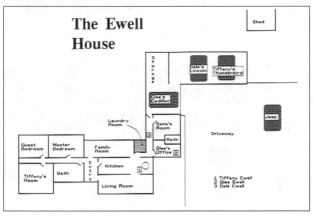

Diagram of the murder scene. Reconstructing the angles and timing of the attacks convinced the Fresno County Sheriff's Department that the Ewells could not have been killed by an ordinary burglar. Evidence later showed that the killer waited alone in the house for most of Easter Sunday, then attacked without warning from the laundry room. *(Diagram by Carlton Smith)*

Fresno County Sheriff's Department Supervising Criminalist Allen Boudreau, holding an AT-9 semiautomatic rifle, modified with a silencer like the one used in the murders. In a long-running series of scientific experiments, Boudreau developed crucial ballistics evidence, including reconstruction of the missing silencer, that tied Joel Radovcich to the murders. *(Photo by Scott Stacy)*

Dana Ewell, on his way to Fresno County Jail, escorted by detectives John Souza, left, and Chris Curtice, right. Dana Ewell repeatedly scorned the two detectives as incompetent during the three-year investigation. *(Photo by Kurt Hegre, reprinted by permission of the* Fresno Bee*)*

Dana Ewell, in jail garb, listens intently to county prosecutors during a pre-trial hearing. His lawyer, Chief Public Defender Peter Jones, watches the judge for reactions. *(Photo by Carlton Smith)*

Joel Radovcich, the alleged hit man, looks back at Dana Ewell as he prepares to go back to jail after a pre-trial hearing. Police allege that Radovcich murdered all three Ewells after Dana Ewell offered him half of the family's $8 million estate. *(Photo by Carlton Smith)*

Peter Jones, Dana Ewell's court-appointed lawyer. Dana Ewell's uncles moved to freeze assets in the Ewell estate to prevent Dana from using any of the money to pay for his defense. That left Dana Ewell, a vociferously conservative critic of government, dependent on the government for his defense. *(Photo by Carlton Smith)*

James Oppliger, Fresno County Chief Deputy District Attorney, and the lead prosecutor in the Ewell murder case. Oppliger was doubtful about the prospects of prosecution until he saw Boudreau's ballistics evidence. *(Photo by Carlton Smith)*

Ed Hunt, Fresno County District Attorney. Hunt twice rejected cases against Dana Ewell before Boudreau's evidence was developed. A casual acquaintance of Dale and Glee Ewell, Hunt now says he wants their son to get the death penalty. *(Photo by Carlton Smith)*

Seen from this perspective, the one-sided conversations were innocuous; certainly, they were in no way conclusively inculpatory. Nowhere in any of these supposed conversations did Joel ever tell Dana Ewell: Listen, pal, I killed your family, now I want your money.

21

The day after these conversations between Joel and Jennifer, May 19, 1993, Joel received a page to call a number at the San Jose Airport. Fifteen minutes later, Dana was observed at the airport. Again, a surveilling officer eavesdropped on Joel's side of the conversation:

"I've been up all night, I haven't slept," Joel was reported to have said.

"I called my guy [at] twelve o'clock at night, he's really serious."

"Okay, maybe so."

"Okay, Dana, okay."

It seemed to the eavesdropper that Joel now told Dana that the Fresno lawyer, Woolf, was going to telephone Jennifer Nunnikoven. And then there was this:

"Someone [is] running around listening to us, or something, I think snitches."

An hour later, Joel called Woolf:

"Okay, Mr. Woolf, they are just trying to trick her or something."

"She doesn't know anything."

"She's so far removed from this thing."

"I can assure you, she knows nothing."

"She's not part of this."

"What if they find me? Can they arrest me? I mean, [on what] statute [?]"

"What happens if it's like on a Friday?"

From this conversation with Woolf, it appears that the proactive strategy of pushing Joel toward panic was having some effect. It seems clear that Joel believed his arrest was imminent.

But expressing fear of arrest, particularly after the events of the preceding weeks, was woefully short of an admission of guilt. In reality, the police had nothing more than suspicions—contacts between Joel and Dana, Joel's unexplained financial resources, and Joel's attempts to circumscribe the detectives' efforts against him through his contacts with Woolf and Jennifer Nunnikoven.

In the latter regard, Joel was at least initially partly successful. The same day Joel assured Woolf that Jennifer knew nothing, that the police were only trying to trick her, Jennifer refused to take the lie detector test. But the following day, Jennifer and her father met with the detectives. This time, Jennifer told investigators of Joel's boasts that he would be a millionaire by the time he was twenty-five.

Throughout the rest of the month, surveilling officers recorded more telephone contacts between Joel and Dana; some of the covert watchers thought Joel seemed "emotionally drained." On May 28, 1993, Joel moved out of his Costa Mesa apartment and returned to his mother's house in the San Fernando Valley. The shadowing team first followed Joel to a restaurant in Ontario, California, about sixty miles east of Los Angeles. Although the detectives did not know this at the time, the restaurant was where Jack Ponce worked.

Five days later, on June 3 at 4:38 P.M., Joel received a page from Jack. This page, coming only seven minutes before another page listing a pay phone number from the San Jose Airport, appears to represent the first time the detectives became even minimally aware of Jack's existence. Eventually the discovery of Jack's relationship with Joel was to have profound consequences for everyone.

At 4:46 P.M., Joel was seen at a pay telephone, presumably in the San Fernando Valley, talking to someone. Nine minutes later, at 4:55 P.M. Dana was seen at a pay phone at the San Jose Airport. Again, portions of Joel's conversation were overheard. The timing of the overheard conversation remains unclear: was it at 4:46 P.M., one minute after Joel had received a page from Jack? Or was it at 4:55 P.M., when the other conversant was presumably Dana? The question of timing seems critical, given the content of the words attributed to Joel:

"What's up? What, what, then why don't they just pick us up?"

"I gotta talk to my guy and we'll see if they can actually charge me with something in that three-shirt deal."

"I was just calling to tell that, I just want us to be extra careful, I mean in line with everything, and whatever, you never know what they hold."

"It's just we gotta hang tough."

The three-shirt deal. But was this conversation with Jack, or was it with Dana? The difference is critical. At that point, because the detectives still had no real knowledge of Jack, it was assumed that Joel had spoken of "that three-shirt deal" with Dana.

But there is support for the idea that the conversation was actually with Jack—first, because Joel was seen at the pay telephone one minute after having received the page from Jack, while Dana was seen at the San Jose telephone *nine minutes later*; and secondly, because it appears from the context that Joel had first called the other party, and was explaining why he had done so:

"I was just calling to tell that, I just want us to be extra careful. . . ."

After all, Jack supposedly knew what had happened at the Ewell house on Easter Sunday; indeed, he was involved in the chain of events himself, wittingly or not. Joel's conversation could easily be interpreted as a warning to Jack: be on the lookout for the police.

"You never know what they hold," he'd said. Seen from an even more sinister perspective, the remark could be interpreted as a reminder to Jack that he was every bit as involved as Joel himself.

It seemed, at least to the detectives, that matters were at last coming to a head. The surveillance on Joel was continued. On June 8, Joel had made a number of telephone calls to a bookstore, along with numerous other pay telephone calls during the first weeks of June.

To them, it seemed that Joel was frustrated about something. It was only later that they learned that Dana had been dipping back into his grandmother's account—$1,500 on June 11, $3,000 more from the same account the next day, when Dana graduated from Santa Clara University.

The surveillance team continued following Joel. On June 15, the covert observers watched as Joel ordered an electronic lock pick, paying $431 for it in money orders. When investigators checked the order, they learned it was to be sent to someone named Jack Ponce. It was the first time detectives heard Jack's name.

Who was this? Further checking of the telephone toll records showed there had been several previous calls between Joel and Jack. Now it appeared to the investigators that Joel was using Jack as a mail drop, as he had done with Tom Duong two years earlier.

And what did Joel want with an electronic lock pick, a device described as a "state-of-the-art" mechanism to open almost any lock? And why was he concealing the name of the actual purchaser?

What was Joel up to now?

On June 24, Joel ordered still more books, again paying with money orders. Detectives decided to check on Joel's reading tastes. That was when they learned the name of the publisher of the books about silencers and booby traps that Joel had supposedly ordered through Tom Duong almost two years earlier.

Paladin Press of Boulder, Colorado, had a reputation for producing off-the-wall titles, virtually all in paperback. The Paladin title catalogue appeared to be a paranoid's bestseller list. With books on how to make silencers, plant bugs, construct bombs, fight dirty, and counterspy, the Paladin catalogue was a wannabe secret agent's information cornucopia. The available titles on how to make silencers caught Souza's attention right away.

Hadn't Boudreau been insisting all along that the murder bullets had come from a gun used with a silencer? And here was Paladin Press, of Boulder, Colorado, offering books on do-it-yourself silencers, and Joel Radovcich was ordering books from Paladin.

But was there any proof that Joel had ordered a book on how to make a silencer? Not from the bookstore, it appeared. Tom Duong had told Burk this was so, but that wasn't irrefutable proof. What about Paladin Press itself? Was it possible they had any records of Joel's purchases of Paladin books at the time when Duong thought the books had been sent to the Duong house—May or June of 1991? Would the order include a book on how to make a silencer?

It was, the detectives decided, worth a shot. Souza made plans to go to Boulder.

Souza arrived in Boulder late in June. It was, he said later, initially a disappointment: Paladin Press had purged its computer system of all old orders.

But wait. It appeared that the publisher kept hard copies of the order forms it received in manila envelopes, one envelope for each day's orders, going back a number of years. Company officials introduced Souza to the stacks of envelopes. He began going through all the envelopes for May and June of 1991, looking for an order from someone named Tom Duong.

"I looked through thousands and thousands of orders," Souza declared later.

It probably seemed like thousands to Souza. But Souza was lucky. There, in the envelope for May 6, 1991, was an order from one Tom Duong, requesting delivery of nearly half a dozen of Paladin's books—including two on the construction of silencers. On the cover of one was a drawing of what appeared to be a high-powered 9 millimeter assault rifle, whose barrel was encased in a long, round, deadly looking tube.

Now it was time for the detectives to take stock. After almost fourteen months of investigation, what did they really have?

It wasn't nothing, but it was close to that. They had three victims, all shot with multiple bullets from a 9-millimeter semiautomatic weapon of some type. They had a large estate, worth as much as $7.5 million to the surviving heir, Dana Ewell. They had the heir acting oddly about the murder of his own family. They had Dana Ewell's relatives, or at least some of them, who were suspicious of him. They had records showing Dana Ewell making large withdrawals from various accounts, including the trust account of his own aged grandmother. They had a series of apparent clandestine contacts between Dana Ewell and an unlikely friend, Joel Radovcich, who seemed to have unexplained sources of money. They had evidence that the Ewell family was murdered with a gun equipped with a silencer, along with evidence that Joel Radovcich was interested in silencers.

Taken together, this circumstantial evidence was suggestive, but no more. While Sergeant Caudill and his investigators were convinced in their own judgment that Dana and Joel had conspired to commit the murders, it wasn't their judgment that counted. That judgment was the responsibility, at least initially, of the Fresno County District Attorney's Office. And lawyers in that office, while intrigued by the threads assembled by the detectives, were unequivocal in their assessment of the case: you don't, the lawyers told the detectives, have nearly enough for us to file charges. Keep working.

Meanwhile, the Ewell estate executor, Michael Dowling, had begun to wonder about Dana Ewell.

"I was aware he had access to large amounts of money," Dowling said of Dana later. There were, for example, the various bank accounts totaling nearly $450,000 that had been turned over to Dana almost immediately after the murders.

Now, by the spring of 1993, Dana and his civil lawyer, Roger Fipps, began pressing Dowling to make a preliminary distribution from the trust to Dana. Dowling contacted the Sheriff's Department to find out the status of the detectives' investigation of the trust's beneficiary.

Would it be proper, Dowling asked the Sheriff's Department, to turn any of the estate proceeds over to Dana, particularly in light of the fact that investigators had publicly declined to rule Dana out as a suspect?

A ranking Sheriff's Department official, Captain Kenneth Hogue, responded in writing to Dowling.

"After lengthy investigation," Hogue wrote, "and with deliberations with the Fresno County District Attorney's Office, it is the position of our department that Dana Ewell is to be considered a prime suspect in the investigation."

22

Jimmie Glee Thurmond and her mother, Mrs. Sargent, were unaware of the mounting suspicion of young cousin Dana out in California. To them, the murders still resounded with incomprehensibility. Why? It was almost impossible to believe that it had happened, let alone to consider who might have been responsible.

In late June 1993, while the detectives were still shadowing Joel Radovcich, Dana and his grandmother traveled to Oklahoma to visit Mrs. Mitchell's sisters, Helen and Grace, and her niece, Jimmie Glee Thurmond. Again, Dana seemed to be the very image of the dutiful grandson; but it was on this trip that Jimmie Glee and Helen were to learn that Big Glee didn't really like her grandson.

"She thought he was ornery," Jimmie Glee recalled later. "Mischievous. He tormented Tiffany all the time." Grandma Glee thought Dana had a bad streak somewhere inside of him; and although she tried to like him, it wasn't easy.

Jimmie Glee and Helen decided to try to get to know Dana better.

"We were trying to accept him as part of the family," Jimmie Glee said later.

He was interested to know where all the oil wells were, so Jimmie Glee took him down to the records office and showed him how to look up all the leases. But when Jimmie

Glee tried to show Dana pictures of young Glee Ewell, when Dana's mother had been cousin Glee living for the summers in Gage, Dana seemed utterly indifferent. It was, Jimmie Glee thought, almost as if, to Dana, his mother had never existed. How odd, Jimmie Glee thought.

23

By the summer of 1993, chief criminalist Allen Boudreau had completed a number of tests on the murder bullets, tests that told him certain things.

One series of examinations showed that the murder bullets did look somewhat like those fired from a Browning 9-millimeter pistol, in they had the same direction of twist (spin) and the same number of lands and grooves (that is, the bullet markings left by the rifling of the barrel) as might have been expected in a Browning pistol.

Still, Boudreau remained convinced that Dale's missing Browning wasn't the murder gun. He knew for sure that no Browning he ever heard of had made those odd scratches. And there was something else a little off about the bullets, Boudreau thought, something subtle that he couldn't quite put his finger on just yet.

Still, investigators were making progress. It seemed almost certain that the bullets used to kill the Ewells had come from inside the house. In a particularly diligent piece of detective work, the son of the owner of Sunnyside Hardware, himself a former police officer, went to his father's house and dug through his father's old business records. Almost unbelievably he emerged with a sales order showing that one Dale Ewell had been the purchaser of a Browning 9-millimeter semiautomatic pistol and two boxes of

9-millimeter bullets in October 1971. The price of the bullets was $7.90 per box.

It therefore seemed quite likely that Dale Ewell, his wife, and his daughter had been killed by the very bullets he'd bought to protect them with, more than twenty years earlier—bullets that his surviving son Dana certainly knew about.

Not long after Souza returned from his trip to Boulder, Boudreau found himself skimming through one of the Paladin publications Souza had brought back with him.

"I was paging through one," he said later, "and it showed a ported barrel. Well, a little lightbulb blinked on. You drill a hole through metal, it leaves a burr on the back side."

Boudreau raced home after work to experiment on his surplus 9-millimeter pistol barrel.

"I chucked the barrel up in a drill vise and a drill press, and I just started drilling holes in it everywhere I could, to get as many as I could in that little short barrel. I got up early the next morning, and was down at work at seven o'clock, in the lab, test-firing it.

"The first bullet down the barrel, there were so many burrs it peeled the jacket off. (Shots) number two through eleven were virtually identical to the murder bullets." The new bullets had the same sort of odd scratches as the slugs found in the walls of the Ewell house. Not only that, the scratches on each of the new bullets were identical to each other—just as the scratches on the Ewell bullets had been. The scratches had been made by the metal burrs left by the porting of the barrels.

Boudreau decided to have a little fun with the detectives. He took one of the new bullets and waited until the detectives were having a conference. Then he slipped into John Souza's office.

"I took that bullet and I set it right in the middle of his desk blotter. Well, it wasn't too long and my office door flies open."

It was Souza, and he was steaming.

"You're going to lose this, and it's evidence," Souza screamed at Boudreau.

"Nah," said Boudreau, "I made that."

"Wait a minute," Souza said. "It looks just like the other ones."

Boudreau dropped new bullets numbers three through eleven on the desk for Souza to see.

It seemed that the mystery of the scratches was now definitely solved. After all, Boudreau had succeed in replicating the scratches himself, by using the porting technique referred to in the silencer book that had been purchased by Joel.

Now the question was: If Boudreau followed *all* of the instructions in the book, would the bullets still look the same?

But building a legitimate silencer—even one for a law-enforcement purpose—isn't easy to do. Boudreau actually had to get permission from the federal government to make one. He had to get a permit!

Boudreau had to fill out forms, get higher-ranking officers to approve, send the forms on to higher-ups at the Bureau of Alcohol, Tobacco and Firearms, and wait for bureaucratic approval. Police agencies aren't exempt from the law, even when they're trying to catch a killer.

When the approval finally came, Boudreau studied the drawings and instructions in the silencer book.

"I tried all kinds of stuff," Boudreau said. The book showed how to construct silencers using cans, metal pipes, and plastic pipes, along with rubber and other insulating materials. A favorite technique was to cut a series of tennis balls in half, hole them to fit them around the gun barrel, then fit the hemispheres end to end in a container of some sort, wrapped with duct tape. The porting of the barrel caused some of the explosive gases to escape into the rubber tennis balls, which acted as a baffle and tended to muffle the noise from the shot.

The book showed various combinations of tennis balls,

steel wool, and other possible baffle materials. Boudreau spent weekends experimenting, trying to make a silencer the way the books outlined.

By the end of the summer, Boudreau had made a silencer using the methods portrayed in the books. He began making test firings of his device and soon realized that when a bullet exited a silencer it carried minute particles of the suppressant materials along with it. It occurred to Boudreau that some traces of those materials might be found in the tape lifts taken from the victims' clothing on the day the bodies were found, and he was right.

Careful examination of some of the murder scene tape lifts showed minute particles of steel wool and rubber—exactly the same as those that emerged from the silencer Boudreau himself had made.

This was hard physical evidence, the kind that would stand up in a court of law. Now the trick would be to somehow connect Joel and/or Dana to a 9-millimeter semi-automatic weapon, and find evidence that either had once made a silencer. If they could only put the right kind of gun in Joel's hands, the investigators reasoned, they might have enough to go all the way.

But how?

24

That same summer, Dana hit Grandmother Glee's account hard, withdrawing $800 on July 1, $2,000 on August 11, $7,000 on August 18, $3,000 on August 30, and another $3,000 on September 29.

Where was all this money going—almost $16,000 that summer alone? Some detectives theorized that, having been balked by Dale and Glee's wills from immediately inheriting, Dana, as trustee for his grandmother, was using his grandmother's account instead.

Detectives went to see Mrs. Mitchell. She complained that Dale never came to visit her. She didn't seem to know anything about the money. But then the detectives learned something that gave them chills. As originally planned, Mrs. Mitchell was to have accompanied Glee and Tiffany to the Easter weekend at Pajaro Dunes. She had changed her mind at the last minute because she hadn't been feeling well.

That meant that Glee Mitchell would likely have returned to the Ewell house with Glee and Tiffany that fateful Sunday . . . in which case, she would have been dead, too.

Dana was furious with the detectives when he found out they visited Glee Mitchell, and he angrily berated the administration of the life-care facility where his grandmother lived. He told them never to permit such a visit again.

In early October, the detectives discovered that Dana was

in San Diego. It appeared to the detectives that Dana was visiting Monica Zent, who was enrolled in law school there. Indeed, as the investigators developed further information about Dana and Monica, they came to the conclusion that Dana was paying for the lease on a condominium for Monica, and was paying her way through law school.

The investigators considered this to be suspicious. After all, Monica had been close to Dana, and had supposedly been with him on the day of the murders. Now Dana appeared to be looting his grandmother's life trust to pay for Monica Zent's education. From life care to life share, some thought, in one easy jump.

It had taken Souza some time to track Jack Ponce down. He found him where he worked, as a bartender in a restaurant in Ontario, California. It had been Ponce, Souza realized, who Joel must have been seeing at the same restaurant on the late May afternoon the surveillance team trailed Joel back to his mother's house.

Souza opened the discussion by asking Jack how well he knew Joel.

Not that well, Jack said. He's my best friend's little brother. I don't socialize with him, if that's what you mean. About the only time I see him is when I happen to be over at Peter's house.

How often is that? Souza asked.

Not that often, said Jack.

Souza had already heard that Jack owned a number of weapons.

What guns do you own? he asked Jack.

He had pistols, Jack said. A rifle. A shotgun.

What kind of pistols?

He had, Jack said, a .44 Charter Arms and a .380 Llama.

Do you own a 9-millimeter?

No, Jack said.

Did Jack ever go shooting with Joel and Peter? Souza asked.

Yes, Jack said. To a gun range a few years ago. Just for fun.

Well, what about this lock pick? Souza asked.

What lock pick? Jack asked.

The one we know you ordered for Joel Radovcich, Souza told him.

Jack was caught. There was only one thing to do. He told Souza he knew of no lock pick; what he'd ordered for Joel was a locksmithing device. He guessed that Joel wanted to study to become a locksmith. The only reason he'd let Joel send it to his address was because Joel moved around a lot and didn't have a permanent place to receive it.

Souza ended the interview soon after, but Jack was badly rattled.

Now the thing that he had been dreading had happened. The police had come to see him, and right away he'd given them reasons to be suspicious of him, Jack thought. How he wished the whole thing would go away!

He'd talked to Joel a couple of times over the summer. Joel was angry at Dana Ewell, Jack thought; Joel complained to Jack that Dana was spending too much money on Monica Zent. Jack got the impression from Joel that Dana was paying for Monica's car, her housing, maybe even her tuition in law school. And here Joel was scraping by on a few hundred dollars here and there. But Jack knew Joel was getting money from somewhere, because he'd resumed his pilot lessons. If he kept on flying, Joel might expect to graduate with a commercial multiengine rating in January 1994.

And what did he, Jack, have? A useless degree that had taken him almost six years to earn, and a job as a bartender. His life was all screwed up, Jack thought; now it looked like it was going to get even worse.

Dana hit Glee Mitchell's account twice more in October, once on October 13 for $1,000 and again on October 25, for $3,000.

Meanwhile, detectives had noticed some construction work going on at the Radovcich family home. Maybe, they reasoned, another Dumpster search would be fruitful. This time, Joel learned of the impending search and asked the company to refuse permission. All that did, of course, was lead the detectives to obtain a search warrant for the Dumpster. While they were at it, in fact, they got one for the Radovcich residence as well.

The search of the Radovcich house took place on October 29, 1993. Among other things it yielded a letter to Joel from the Fresno lawyer Terrence Woolf, dated April 8, 1993, and acknowledging the receipt of a $3,000 retainer fee. The investigators checked their records. The day after the fee was paid, Dana had withdrawn $7,000 from his grandmother's trust.

After the search, Souza, Allen Boudreau, and crime scene technician Jack Duty adjourned to Boudreau's hotel room. For almost ten hours that afternoon and evening, the three men discussed the case.

"We went back to the crime scene," Boudreau said, "and we started talking about everything, and started making notes. We went up to dinnertime, went out to dinner, talked through dinner, came back, and went up until about eleven o'clock. Came up with a bunch of ideas, little things, really. I mean we were down to scratching for anything."

It seemed increasingly clear that the key to solving the case would lie in the weapon. Neither Dana nor Joel had shown any real signs of cracking. Monica Zent wouldn't help. She had already declined to be interviewed. Peter Radovcich and the rest of the Radovcich family were barely cooperative. If they could only find out what sort of weapon had been used. If they could only find a way to show that Joel had access to the same type of weapon, then the pieces might start falling together.

More and more, Souza was starting to feel that Jack Ponce was a key to the puzzle. Jack was friends with Joel and Peter. Jack was a gun nut, it appeared. *If I were Joel and I wanted an untraceable gun, what would I do?* Souza wondered. *I might steal one, but that would be risky. It would be better to get someone to buy one for me—someone I could trust. And someone willing to do it, no questions asked.*

Someone, Souza decided, like Jack Ponce.

25

Souza and the other investigators spent the next few weeks learning about Jack Ponce. He didn't seem a very impressive figure, they thought. Certainly he wasn't the type to be the mastermind of any criminal plot, even if he was two years older than Joel and Dana. Indeed, Jack seemed like the sort of person other people might push around.

The investigators learned that Jack had taken six years to graduate from UCLA, which seemed to show that he was a little less than motivated. He seemed to be naturally attracted to the path of least resistance, even a bit lazy. If anything, Jack was a follower, not a leader. All in all, he seemed the perfect choice to be a dupe's dupe.

In checking Jack's previous addresses, the investigators learned that for a period in early 1992, Jack had gone through a rough time financially when his father had refused to pay Jack's bills anymore.

But before this, Jack's father had paid for an apartment in Santa Monica, which Jack had shared with several other students. It took time, but eventually investigators were able to interview those roommates of Jack. The investigators discovered that Jack hadn't used his room in the apartment in the summer of 1991.

Why not? the detectives asked.

He was staying in San Bernardino with his mother, the

detectives were told. Somebody else used his room.

Who was that?

His best friend's little brother. Someone named Joel.

Joel Radovcich.

On December 8, Souza went to San Bernardino to reinterview Jack Ponce. He caught up with Jack in front of his mother's house.

Souza demanded to know why Jack hadn't told him that Joel Radovcich had subleased his apartment in the summer of 1991.

I don't recall that Joel ever moved in, Jack said. In fact, I'm still not sure whether he did or not.

Well, did he pay you anything? Souza asked.

Yes. No. I don't know.

Well, when did you go shooting with Peter and Joel?

I never went shooting with Joel, Jack said.

Yes, you did. You told us that the last time we talked.

No, I didn't. I've never been shooting with Joel. Just Peter. And about that lock pick. Joel had it sent to my address because Peter's wife would've gotten mad about it. And it was locksmithing equipment, that's all it was.

Have you seen either Joel or Peter since the last time we talked?

No, Jack said.

Well, I'll tell you what, Souza said. Would you be willing to take a lie detector test, about what you know about Joel and Peter?

Of course, Jack said.

Good, said Souza. Because we've got one all set up. We can do it right now.

Now? No, I won't do it, Jack said.

Why not?

I just don't want to, that's all, Jack told them.

Jack's lying to us, Souza told the other investigators. I know he is. I'll bet you anything he was the one that got a 9-millimeter for Joel Radovcich. And I'm going to prove it.

*   *   *

Jack was feeling terrible. In the short time since the detectives had first come to see him in October, he'd already lost nearly twenty-five pounds, and he wasn't that heavy to begin with.

Jack's father noticed his son's depression. The sudden weight loss made Jack's father believe Jack might have developed AIDS. When Jack's father assured him that the family would stand by him if that were the case, Jack said that wasn't the trouble at all. The police were what was depressing him.

The police? Jack's father knew nothing about any of this. What did the police want from Jack?

It's Peter, Jack said. Peter's little brother has got himself involved in a Menendez-type deal.

Menendez? Did Jack mean murder? A family murder, where the parents were killed by the sons?

Jack nodded.

Nor were things going well for Peter Radovcich. After a few rocky years, the end had finally come with Danielle. She and Peter separated around December 1, 1993. By March 1994, following another earthquake, Peter would return to live at his mother's house in West Hills.

26

Early in January of the New Year, Boudreau was again gazing at the murder bullets. He was virtually certain he'd identified the cause of the odd scratches on the sides. He'd built his own silencer, to specifications listed in the silencer book, and all of the bullets fired through the Boudreau silencer left the same sort of side markings as the murder bullets.

Now, at the suggestion of Carlo Rosati, Boudreau looked at the bottom of the bullets—the part that fitted into the shell casing. There, for the first time, Boudreau noticed still more unusual scratches. He looked at the rest of the murder bullets. Only one other of those had similar markings.

What was going on here? What had made those markings? Why were they on some of the bullets, and not on the rest? Boudreau disassembled the eighteen remaining bullets that were still in the $7.90 box. Six of the eighteen unused bullets had the markings—the same ratio as the two out of six murder bullets, one out of three.

Boudreau didn't know what to think—except that, as things were developing, this would be the most interesting case he'd ever worked on, one little puzzle after another, all inside a bigger riddle.

In the middle of February, Souza and Chris Curtice made another trip to Southern California. First they talked with Jack Ponce's father.

Dr. Ernest Ponce said he knew what the detectives wanted. He'd talked to Jack about it, he said. Jack was worried sick, he added. But Jack's father assured the detectives Jack wasn't involved. When he'd thought Jack was suffering from AIDS because of his abrupt weight loss, Jack had told him about Peter's brother, and the "Menendez-type deal."

Three days later, Souza and Curtice talked to Jack once more.

They began by asking him once again whether he'd ever owned a 9-millimeter gun.

Yes, I did, Jack said. Once.

What kind was it?

It was an AT9, Jack said. A rifle. Had a folding stock.

Why didn't you tell us that the first time we talked?

I did, Jack said. I told you the first time we talked I had a rifle. You guys just weren't listening.

Jack produced a tape recorder. You keep telling me I said things I didn't say, he said. From now on, I'm going to have a record.

The detectives produced their own tape recorder.

All right. Tell us about this 9-millimeter rifle. It was an AT9, you said?

Yes, Jack said. I bought it for my birthday two years ago.

Where is it now?

It was stolen, Jack said.

Stolen? When?

It was stolen from my car. I filed a police report on it.

When was it stolen?

Sometime in the fall of 1992, Jack said. I was going to UCLA at the time.

Why'd you want this rifle?

I wanted a long gun because it was more accurate. I wanted to shoot opossums with it. They'd been getting into my mom's attic.

The attic! Souza and Curtice couldn't believe their ears. Here was Jack trying to tell them his stolen 9-millimeter rifle had been used to hunt opossums in his mother's attic. Such outright dissembling was a sure sign that Jack was getting ready to crack.

Had he ever fired the gun?

Yes, Jack said. He'd taken it up to a canyon behind his house and fired off ten rounds. He didn't like it because it was too loud, he said.

Did Joel ever shoot the gun?

No, Jack said.

Did you ever lend it to anyone?

No.

Well, did Joel ever even *see* this gun?

"No, no," Jack said.

"Mr. Ponce," Souza said, "you never talked to Peter or Joel over the phone and let them know you had this gun?"

No, said Jack. He was going to tell Peter about it, but then thought he'd surprise him.

"I was going to sneak up and grab Pete and take him. But I guess he wasn't meant to be a 'possum killer," Jack said.

Well, said Souza, did anyone suggest to you that you buy this gun?

"No," Jack said. "I saw it in a magazine. No one suggested it to me."

Did you ever tell anyone that you had that gun?

"I want to think that over," Jack said. "I don't want you guys to say I was inconsistent with my story."

Well, Souza said, where did you keep this gun from the time you got it to the time you say it was stolen?

He'd moved it around, Jack said. Sometimes he had it at his girlfriend's apartment, sometimes he had it at his mother's house in San Bernardino. Then he'd put it into the trunk of his car. That's where it was when it was stolen.

Besides that electronic lock pick, the detectives said, did you ever purchase anything else for Joel?

"Uh, no," Jack said. "I'm trying to think really hard if I can remember anything."

Anyway, Jack added, if he'd known it was a lock pick,

he never would have agreed to do it for Joel.

But, Souza continued, you told us that you and Joel and Peter went to a gun range and shot, didn't you?

No, Jack said. I told you Peter and I went to a range and shot.

Souza: You told us the first time Joel went with you.

Jack: He went with us, but when the range master wanted his identification, Joel wouldn't give it, so he left without shooting.

Souza: Do you have any idea of why Joel might be avoiding us?

Jack: "I don't know why he wouldn't talk to you, if he wasn't involved or something. It seems odd to me."

The detectives then told Jack that the Ewells were killed with a 9-millimeter gun. They were pretty sure, the detectives said, that Joel Radovcich had killed the Ewells; and that it was possible Joel had used Jack's gun.

If Joel did it, and he used an AT9, Jack said, it wasn't mine.

With that the interview was concluded. But Souza and Curtice were elated. They were closing in, they were sure of it. Neither detective believed Jack for a minute when he'd said Joel had never seen or fired the gun, or even knew about it. Jack was lying, he had to be.

The following day, a Saturday, they called Fresno and asked to talk to Boudreau. Boudreau was home, in his garage, still drilling holes in gun barrels.

Souza and Curtice told Boudreau they'd talked to Ponce, and that Jack had confirmed that he had once owned a 9-millimeter rifle, one called an AT9. Now, the detectives said, they were on their way to the gun store in Northridge where Jack had said he had bought it.

They'd be there in an hour or so. What should they look for to see if it was the same sort of gun as the one used in the murders?

"Okay," Boudreau told Souza, "here's what you do, bud. If they've got one of these guns there, get the gun. Put a flashlight or some sort of light source at the receiver, and look down the barrel. It should have six lands and grooves, with a right-hand twist.''

The store did have an AT9, and Souza did as Boudreau had directed. He called Boudreau back.

''Yep,'' Souza said. Six lands and grooves, with a right-hand twist. The AT9 met all the requirements to be the murder weapon.

''Great,'' said Boudreau. ''Buy it and bring it back.''

Souza couldn't do that without the approval of Sheriff Magarian. Instead he told the gun store proprietor not to sell the rifle to anyone, that the Fresno County Sheriff's Department would be back to pick it up—along with the sales slip for the gun Jack Ponce had bought. The date on the sales slip was March 23, 1992, and the gun had been picked up by Ponce on April 8, 1992—eleven days before the murders.

In the following week, Jack drove to the San Fernando Valley. He went to the Radovcich family home. He played some basketball with Joel and his brothers. Later, he played the tape he had made of Souza and Curtice's questions, and his answers.

So what? So what if the cops thought they knew what sort of gun had been used? So what if Jack once had such a gun? It didn't prove anything. They didn't have the gun, and they never would, would they?

Right.

27

I t didn't take Boudreau very long to discover that the land-and-groove impressions made on bullets fired from the AT9 Souza had bought matched the lands and grooves on the murder bullets. If an AT9 was the murder weapon, it would leave impressions virtually indistinguishable from those he had been staring at for so many months.

But here is the hard nut of forensic science: all that could be said of the AT9 was that it could not be excluded as the sort of gun that had been used. It was not possible to say that it was the *only* sort of gun that could have been used. At least, not yet.

Still, another large piece of the puzzle now appeared to be in place. In the Ewell estate, the detectives had motive, for Dana. In the lack of alibi for Joel on the day of the murders, they had, by inference, opportunity. Now, with Jack's connection to Joel and the admission that he'd once owned a 9-millimeter rifle, they had the beginnings of means. Motive, Opportunity, Means—the three pillars of any criminal investigation.

The question was: Could the detectives prove Jack's AT9 had somehow made it into Joel's hands—and before April 19, 1992?

With their suspicions against Jack Ponce now hardened, Souza and Curtice set about trying to break his story. They were sure he'd somehow passed the supposedly stolen rifle on to Joel. If they could only get him to admit it they could crack the case.

They tracked down the burglary report Jack had filed, the one in which he'd said that the AT9 was stolen from the trunk of his car. No one in the Los Angeles Police Department had actually looked at Jack's car to see if it had really been broken into. Jack had simply filled out a form in October 1992, saying that the gun had been in the trunk and that it had been taken. He suggested that his girlfriend's roommate might have been responsible for the theft.

The detectives visited Jack's girlfriend. Jack had never shown her a semiautomatic assault rifle, the girlfriend told the detectives. In fact, she'd be surprised if Jack ever had such a gun; an assault rifle didn't seem to be his style. After the burglary of his car, Jack had never mentioned to her that a rifle had been taken.

The detectives went back to see Jack one more time.

Souza began by describing to Jack exactly what had happened in the Ewell house—how Tiffany had been shot in the back of the head without warning, how Glee had run for her life, and how Dale, coming in an hour later, had the front of his face blown out by a bullet from behind.

"We don't feel you had anything to do with these murders," Souza told Jack. But, Souza continued, they were pretty sure that Joel had used Jack's missing gun to commit the crimes.

Now, Souza said, Jack had a choice: he could be a hero for helping solve the crimes, or he could be a chump.

"We need you to tell us you bought this gun for Joel," Souza told Jack.

I didn't, Jack said. You're wrong.

Souza: You should talk to us, to eliminate yourself as a suspect. You could be charged as an accessory to murder.

Jack: I don't know anything about it.

Souza was beginning to lose his patience.

Look, he said, let me run the scenario down to you, just to let you know where you're at:

If we find out you're involved, we're going to get a warrant for your arrest, and you're going to be charged as a third conspirator in a triple murder case. If you're convicted, you could be looking at the death penalty. Don't you get it? This is your last chance.

I have nothing to do with it, Jack said.

Souza sighed. Sometimes, he knew, it was remarkable how stupid people could be.

28

Two long blocks south of the Fresno County Sheriff's Department, and separated from it by the odd-looking courthouse known as the Pigeon Coop, stands a tall, square, blocklike building that was once constructed as the city of Fresno's largest office complex. There, on the tenth floor of the seventeen-story tower, were the offices of District Attorney Ed Hunt, and most of his 160 subordinate lawyers.

It was, Hunt was to recall later, sometime in early March 1994 that detectives from the Sheriff's Department asked for a meeting. Hunt and two of his top assistants, Ken Hahus and Jim Oppliger, listened impassively as Sergeant Caudill and Detectives Souza, Burk, and Curtice told why they wanted the District Attorney's Office to file murder charges against Dana Ewell, Joel Radovcich, and Jack Ponce.

The detectives sketched in the circumstantial evidence: Dana's reported obsession with money, his manipulative background, his uncles' doubts about his character and motives; his frequent contacts with Joel Radovcich, his odd reaction to Curtice's news that detectives believed Radovcich had murdered Dana's family, his refusal to cooperate with investigators; the overheard statements made by Joel while on the pay telephones, including the reference to the "three-shirt deal"; Joel's unexplained income; his unverifiable alibi; Joel's interest in silencers and guns; his ordering of the electronic lock pick through Jack Ponce; Jack Ponce's purchase of a 9-millimeter rifle, indistinguishable from the type of weapon that had been used to commit the murders; and, finally, the fact that the rifle had supposedly been stolen, although no one but Jack ever seemed to be aware that he'd even had it.

Those were facts, said the detectives; and the facts, when combined with the circumstances of the murders, pointed in only one direction: that Dana Ewell had hired Joel Radovcich to murder the Ewell family, and that Joel had somehow prevailed on his brother's best friend, Jack Ponce, to procure the weapon used in the crime.

Who knew the Ewell family would be arriving home separately that Easter Sunday? Dana did. Who knew the code to turn off the alarm? Dana. Who knew there would be 9-millimeter bullets in the house, and where to find them, along with a pistol that might be taken in an attempt to throw police off the track? Dana. Who had prepared an alibi, right down to saving his nickel-and-dime receipts, and making sure to be with the family of an FBI agent? Dana. Who stood to inherit all the millions? Dana.

Who was being such pals with Dana after the murders? Joel. Who had sources of unexplained income? Joel. Who had ordered books on making silencers? Joel. Who had no verifiable alibi on the day of the crimes? Joel. Who had boasted he would be a millionaire by the time he was twenty-five because he had "a cop-proof plan?" Joel.

Who had bought a 9-millimeter rifle, with the same number of lands and grooves, the same right-hand twist as the murder weapon? Jack. Whose gun had supposedly been stolen? Jack. Who was friends with Joel, who had once sublet him an apartment? Jack.

Dana, Joel, and Jack.

It was plain as day what had happened, the detectives said. Three callow kids, all rich, all from well-to-do families, had conspired to murder the Ewell family so that Dana could get the money for himself. Doubtless he was planning to pay the others off, and it appeared that he'd already started, at least with Joel.

But the art of detection is wholly different from the art of prosecution. The investigator's job is to divine the answers, to establish the facts. The prosecutor's job is different. The prosecutor isn't interested in answers as much as proof. The arenas are completely different, and, often, it is difficult for the inhabitants of one world to see the conditions of the other.

We believe you, Hahus and Oppliger told the detectives. We're sure you're right. The problem is, there's just not enough evidence. A good defense attorney will rip this case to shreds if it ever gets into court. There are a thousand reasonable explanations for all your facts, and nine hundred ninety-nine of them are innocent explanations. You guys have to find out what happened; we have to prove it beyond a reasonable doubt, and right now you've still got too much doubt.

If we were to file charges on these three guys, Hahus and Oppliger said, and the case went to trial, and we were to lose—don't get mad, but there's a good chance of that— then we'd never be able to try these guys for this crime, ever again. They could walk, completely. Then you will have wasted all your time, and ours, and, even worse, the bad guys will be out on the streets living it up.

Well, said the detectives, what more do we need?

You need more evidence, the prosecutors said—like something that will show that of all the people in the world, *only* these three guys could have done it. Something solid. You're not there yet.

Souza, for one, was bitter, and also frustrated. He *knew* what the story was—he was the one who'd talked to Dana Ewell, Joel Radovcich, and Jack Ponce. He was the one who'd looked into their eyes, who'd seen the lies and evasions, not the damn lawyers.

He'd spent hundreds of hours on the telephone, driven thousands of miles, worked huge amounts of overtime on the case. His home life was going to wrack and ruin under the stress. He had begun to hate Dana Ewell, the rich little snot, with his sneering jokes about Mutt and Jeff, looking down his nose at Souza and everybody else who worked for a living.

Well, what was he going to do about it? Sit around and gripe that the lawyers were too dumb to know one end of a cow from the other? Souza's wife prodded him.

"She challenged me," he said later. So Souza sighed, and went back to work.

29

It would be interesting to know whether word of this decision not to file charges somehow filtered back to Dana
and Joel during the early part of 1994. Certainly they
seem to have acted as if they knew the pressure was off.

In the middle of March, they flew together to Mexico in
Dana's expensive new airplane. Detectives watched them
fly off, doubtless wondering whether they would come
back; or whether Joel would, at least. The answer came
several days later, when Dana and Joel both flew into
Fresno Air Terminal. Surveilling detectives followed them,
and this time Dana stopped his car and advanced on the
detectives in apparent anger.

Meanwhile, the murder bullets and the bullets still remaining in the ammunition box were sent to the FBI. That
had been one of the ideas discussed by Souza, Jack Duty,
a crime scene specialist, and Boudreau the previous fall at
the day-and-night session at the hotel. The metal in the
bullets could be subjected to neutron-activation analysis to
determine the specific metallic content. If the murder bullets
had the same content as the bullets in the box, it would be
strong evidence that the fatal bullets indeed had come from
those found in the house.

"We needed to link that ammunition up to the box,"
Boudreau said afterward.

"Because, if the ammunition in the box was used, and

we knew the Browning wasn't used—I mean, *I* was sure of it—then that meant whoever did the killings had known about that ammunition and relied on it. You wouldn't go in there with a loaded gun and think, 'Oh, here's some free ammo, I think I'll unload these, and load these [instead]. If you wanted the ammo, you'd just stick it in your pocket. But if you're waiting to kill some people . . . well, there's no way around that. Anybody can argue anything, but there's no logical way around the fact that the killer had to have known those bullets were there beforehand.''

On March 21, 1994, the FBI test results were delivered. The analysis showed that the murder slugs had indeed come from the same batch of lead used to make the unused bullets found in the opened box. The killer used those bullets. Now the question was: How could he be sure they would be there on the day of the murders?

With the decision not to seek charges, another decision was also made: the surveillance of Joel and Dana, intermittent throughout the year, was finally scaled back.

Altogether, the rolling teams had filed hundreds of pages of reports on the activities of both Joel and Dana, and documented well over sixty telephone contacts and meetings—all at a tremendous cost of time and money. On one of the occasions, an eavesdropping plainclothes officer said he'd overheard Joel chiding Dana—suggesting that Dana come to visit him, and bring ''the whole family'' with him. If the other conversant was indeed Dana, this was either the worst sort of black humor, or it was a not-too-subtle dig that Dana owed Joel. At the very least it showed that the conspirators, if that's who was talking, were cold-blooded in the extreme.

Yet, in terms of proof, the best that could be said of this monumental surveillance effort was that it produced only circumstantial evidence—and evidence that was equivocal, at that.

So Joel and Dana had met one another, and talked frequently—so what? What did it prove?

That they knew each other? That they spent time in each

other's company, or in telephone conversations?

Even if Dana had given money to Joel—what did that really prove? He'd given money to Monica, too. Did anyone really think Monica was part of some sort of conspiracy? Wasn't this just one way Dana had to show off again—as with the limousine, or buying everyone hamburgers?

Indeed, the anti-argument might easily be made that the very fact Joel and Dana had frequent, easily documented contact with one another showed that neither had anything to feel guilty about—that they were acting no different than any other two people who were innocent might also act.

That they discussed the case with each other was perfectly reasonable, given that both their names had been publicly linked as possible suspects in the crime.

In the winter of this disappointment, the detectives were forced to wonder:

Was it possible Joel was right, after all? Was the plan, if it even existed, truly a "cop-proof plan"?

As the spring of 1994 unfolded, it began to be increasingly apparent that there would be only one way to tie Dana, Joel, and Jack to the crimes: the detectives would have to prove that Joel Radovcich had once had possession of Jack Ponce's Featherlight AT9 assault rifle; that he had modified the rifle with a silencer; and that he had used that same rifle on the very day that the murders had been committed.

But how? Neither Dana nor Joel, nor even Jack, appeared willing to say any of this was so. And the gun was, apparently, long gone at this point, either stolen as Jack kept insisting, or, alternatively, so well hidden by Joel that it might never be found.

But the investigators concluded that finding the *actual* gun might not be essential.

What would happen, the detectives brainstormed, if a gun *almost exactly identical* to Jack's missing AT9 were modified with the same sort of silencer Joel might have made, using the Paladin book? Would a gun with virtually the same characteristics leave the same markings as those found on the murder bullets? What if a number of guns were modified in similar ways, and only the AT9 left the right sort of markings?

Wouldn't that be evidence that the gun used to kill the Ewells was an AT9 Featherlight—just exactly the sort of gun Joel's good friend Jack claimed had been stolen, although no one but Jack had ever seen it?

Wouldn't that be enough to put the detectives over the top?

It was a shot, some thought. It was a shot worth taking. As a result, the investigation entered a new phase, one almost completely concerned with Allen Boudreau, the science of forensics, and the arcana of ballistics.

That same summer, a final bit of bad luck caught up with Austin Ewell. His deep grief at the death of his oldest son had given way first to anger, then to certainty: Dana had to be behind the murders, Austin was convinced. The little kid had always been a rotten person, spoiled bad by Glee, Austin thought; when Dale and his family came to visit, Dale helped around the farm, but not Dana. It was almost as if he wasn't a Ewell.

It was strange Dana never came to see him, Austin thought—not even after the murders had Dana come to visit. He doesn't want to face me, Austin thought. He doesn't want to look me in the eye and tell me he doesn't know what happened to his father, my son.

Unlike Dana, Austin thought, he and Dale, and all the real Ewells had worked all their lives. Nobody gave them anything; they earned what was theirs. Work was life, and it had always been that way.

So it was fitting, in a way, that Austin Ewell was hard at work one night, in August 1994, when a generator exploded, killing the father of Dale Ewell instantly. He had worked all his life, and in the end his work had killed him, just as it had his son.

30

That spring of 1994, Boudreau had received a new permit to build a silencer from the federal Bureau of Alcohol, Tobacco and Firearms. Having obtained an AT9 from the same store where Jack Ponce had obtained his stolen rifle, the Sheriff's Department had a unique opportunity to see whether the marks on the murder bullets could be duplicated.

This silencer would be based on the specifications contained in the Paladin book—the one that showed an AT9-like rifle on the cover, modified with what appeared to be a thick black tube, obviously a silencer.

The Paladin book was fairly specific.

Construction of a noise suppressor, was, of course, against federal law. Indeed, it was against the law to make such a device in most countries of the world. Nevertheless, Paladin's [anonymous] author provided step-by-step specifics.

The theory behind a silencer, or noise suppressor, is fairly simple. The noise of a gunshot is produced by two simultaneous effects: the expansion of gases exploding down the barrel, which propel a bullet; both the gases and the bullet strike the surrounding air, producing a shock wave, similar to a thunderclap.

By venting some of the gases into a receptacle, the shock wave from the gases is lessened and, occasionally, the speed of the bullet may be reduced to a subsonic velocity. The trick lies in determining how much gas to vent, and in constructing an effective sound receptacle. Vent too much gas and the bullet won't move; design an ineffective receptacle, and the barrel might crack and the receptacle blow up.

The venting is accomplished by drilling a series of holes in the side of the gun barrel—"porting." The sound receptacle is constructed by wrapping the vented barrel in a wire mesh or other similar material, then enclosing the mesh in a pipe or tube. The vented gases flow into the mesh, thus reducing the shock wave. The number of venting holes and the size of the receptacle depends on the type of ammunition used.

One of the silencers depicted in the Paladin book was designed for a 9-millimeter rifle. Making this silencer first required the disassembly of the barrel from the rest of the rifle, which in the case of the AT9 Featherlight was easily accomplished, since the barrel unscrewed from the stock. Next a large washer, about two and one half inches, was to be welded around the barrel to anchor the suppressor.

After a series of holes were drilled in the barrel, the barrel was to be surrounded by steel wool and tennis balls that had been cut in half, and inserted into a length of PVC pipe glued to the washer. The assembly was then to be capped with a PVC end, with a hole drilled in the cap to permit the exit of the bullet. After assembly, the pipe was to be tightly wrapped in duct tape to help prevent cracking from the heat of the gases.

With the AT9 procured by Souza from the Northridge gun store, Boudreau began manufacturing the silencer as described by the Paladin book. That way, the investigators would be able to determine whether the markings left on test bullets would be the same as those left on the murder bullets.

But would this be enough? There might, in fact, be another way to establish that the weapon used to murder the Ewells was the one purchased by Jack Ponce.

As it happens, while they may look the same, no two gun barrels are exactly identical. Cast from a single piece of hardened steel, most barrels are turned by machining a core from the interior. Once the core is removed, another tool machines the rifling—the lands and grooves. Over time, the rifling tool changes slightly, because of the wear. As a result, minute differences in the rifling of each barrel occur over time.

In other words, a rifle barrel made when the rifling tool is new is likely to be slightly different in characteristics than a barrel made when the tool has been used for some time. The differences will be apparent in the rifling marks left by each barrel on the bullets fired through it.

Therefore, rifling marks left on a bullet fired by a barrel manufactured at about the same time as the barrel of the gun bought by Jack Ponce should be more similar to the marks left on the murder bullets than a barrel made much before or after.

But how to find a barrel made at almost the same time as Jack's barrel?

There was a way, Souza discovered. It was tedious, however.

Souza began the search with the sales order on Jack's gun. That gun, sold March 23, 1992, had a serial number of A92407. Souza then called Feather Industries in Colorado. Would it be possible, he asked, for the company to provide him with the names and telephone numbers of wholesalers who had purchased AT9s in 1992, along with the serial numbers for those weapons?

Feather Industries produced the list, and Souza began the work of trying to track down the wholesalers, and from them the retailers who had sold the guns. Soon Souza was up to his elbows in gun dealers, telephone numbers and serial numbers, and, eventually, the individual purchasers of the weapons.

While Souza was keeping the telephone lines occupied, Boudreau began to examine the AT9 murder and test bullets all over again.

Boudreau now looked closer at the land-and-groove impressions on the sides of the AT9 bullets. These markings formed a helix pattern as they scored the copper jacket as the bullet turned on its way out of the barrel. But these land-and-groove impressions seemed a little off, to Boudreau. They weren't quite the same as the markings on most of the other 9-millimeter bullets he'd tested since the case began. The direction of twist might be the same as in a normal 9-millimeter, but it appeared that the rate of twist was slower.

How could that be? It was only a slight difference, but the more Boudreau looked at the bullets, the more convinced he was that the length of the twist was different in the AT9 bullets than in most conventional weapons. Where most 9-millimeter barrels had a complete twist in ten inches of barrel length, the AT9 slugs appeared to have a slightly longer twist. The lands and grooves seemed to be slightly more elongated than those in ordinary 9-millimeter test bullets, and the difference seemed to be in the helical angles of the land-and-groove impressions.

"You're talking about less than one degree [difference in the helical angle] in a mark that's less than one two-hundred-thousandths of an inch long," Boudreau said later. "I had to do some serious problem solving."

Boudreau devised an experiment to test his hypothesis. Afterward, he refused to disclose exactly how his experiment was conducted, except to say that it involved some complicated mathematics. But the result was clear: it was apparent that the AT9 barrel had one twist in twelve inches, not the normal one-in-ten twist.

The murder bullets had one twist in twelve; so did the bullets from the test AT9. Did any other gun manufacturers have a similar one-in-twelve twist? Try as Boudreau might, he couldn't find any other gun with an identical ratio. It seemed almost certain that the gun that had been used to slaughter the Ewell family had been an AT9.

Then, in August, Souza hit pay dirt. He tracked down the owners of several different AT9s.

Hey, Souza told them over the telephone, and sounding a bit like a used-car salesman, have I got a deal for you! How would you like to have a brand-new gun barrel for your AT9—absolutely free of charge!

Two of the gun owners agreed to the swap. One of them was the owner of barrel number A92406—the one manufactured just before Jack Ponce's gun. That was about as close as the detectives would ever come to the actual murder ballistics, short of having the Ponce gun itself.

Boudreau modified A92406 according to the Paladin silencer book, and test-fired it. The test bullets looked exactly like those used in the murders.

At last, this was hard evidence—almost akin to a DNA test. With the test bullets virtually indistinguishable from the murder bullets, it was certain beyond any reasonable doubt that the gun used to murder Dale, Glee, and Tiffany Ewell was the gun purchased by Jack Ponce.

31

Just when it appeared that Boudreau had proved the case, he was assailed with self-doubts.

He thought he'd done everything correctly. But, he told himself, *What the heck do I know about this? I've never made a silencer before this. And what if there's something I've overlooked, some assumption I've made that can't be proved? What then? The whole case goes down the tubes, and it'll be my fault.*

For some months, ever since he'd found the unusual markings at the base of the bullets in January, Boudreau had wanted to go to the Winchester ammunition plant in East Alton, Illinois. He wanted to see if the Winchester people had any idea of what had made the odd marks on the base of the bullets.

Because two of the six murder bullets had the base marks, and six of the eighteen in the ammunition box also had the marks—a ratio of one out of three—Boudreau had the idea that something in the manufacturing process had caused the marks. Maybe, he reasoned, the number of such bullets were exceedingly small. That would be additional evidence that the bullets used to kill the Ewells had come from the ammunition found in the house. In turn, that would help show that the killer had to have inside information.

Boudreau's superiors weren't that enthusiastic about a

trip to East Alton, Illinois. Is it absolutely required? they asked.

Well, no, Boudreau said. I'd just feel a bit more comfortable if I knew what made those marks. And in fact, if you really want to know, I'd feel a lot better if someone checked all of my work, just to be sure. A second opinion can't do any harm.

Or could it? At least at this point, the detectives had something solid to base their case on; certainly Boudreau's findings—the silencer replication, the virtually identical ballistics impressions, the one-in-twelve twist—those were enough to justify a warrant for the arrest of Joel and Jack, and likely, also Dana. Clearly, Dana would be hard-pressed to explain why a gun once owned by his friend Joel's pal Jack Ponce was used to kill his family.

But what if an outside expert came up with different conclusions? Then the Sheriff's Department would be stuck with that different opinion, and would sooner or later have to disclose the fact that an outside expert disagreed with Boudreau. It was a gamble.

That fall, Sheriff Magarian decided to accept Boudreau's recommendation for a second opinion. Boudreau knew just who he wanted to check his work—Arizona gun expert Lucien Haag, often used as an expert witness. It was Haag, for example, who provided expert testimony in the Ruby Ridge case in Idaho involving survivalist Randy Weaver.

In October, Boudreau, Souza, and Lieutenant Wiley personally drove Boudreau's silencers, test results, and the murder bullets to Scottsdale, Arizona. Lucien Haag agreed to replicate all of Boudreau's tests to determine the scientific validity of Boudreau's conclusions. It doesn't matter how much it costs, Haag was told. We have to know if these conclusions are right or wrong.

Haag set to work, but not before making a few suggestions: the detectives might want to check with Feather Industries to determine who made the gun barrels, and further check with the gun-barrel maker to see if Boudreau's one-twist-in-twelve analysis was accurate. It might also help to collect the rifling button used to tool the suspect barrel, because the tool itself might prove to be definitive evidence as to the source of the land-and-groove impressions on the murder bullets.

Oh, Haag said, one more thing: Boudreau might profit from a trip to the Winchester plant at East Alton, Illinois.

In November 1994, Boudreau and Souza set off to East Alton, and points farther east. At the Winchester ammunition factory, Boudreau and Souza were shown the entire bullet manufacturing process, from the blocks of lead used to make the bullets to the machinery used to fashion the lead cores, the copper jackets, the brass cartridge casings, and the assembly process.

The unusual markings on one out of three of the murder bullets were quickly recognized by the Winchester officials. The marks were caused by a worn coning punch—the machine that punched down every 1.6 seconds to crimp the edges of the copper jacket just before the fitting into the cartridge casing.

Boudreau had the ammunition box with him. Based on the coding inside the box, the Winchester officials concluded that the ammunition had indeed been made in early 1971. Generally, the coning punches and other equipment were checked between each manufacturing shift. As a result, very few bullets would have been manufactured with the unusual markings on the bullet base.

How many bullets? Boudreau asked.

Not much more than 7,500, the Winchester officials said.

As far as Boudreau was concerned, that clinched it. If only 7,500 bullets might have been made with the worn coning punch in early 1971, what were the chances that six of those bullets would still be around more than twenty years after they were made? The odds that two different bullet buyers might have each had bullets with the odd markings but made from the same block of lead, *more than twenty years* after the bullets were made, were impossibly high. The bullets had to have been in the house before the murders, there could be no further question about it.

From East Alton, Boudreau and Souza traveled to Philadelphia, where Souza made two new AT9 barrel acquisitions; and then to New Hampshire and the Green Mountain Barrel Company. The Green Mountain company had made the 1992 barrels for Feather Industries. Indeed, they had made only 514 barrels before the date of the murders, and most of these, according to Feather Industries, had gone on to distributors on the East Coast. And here Boudreau also discovered that his helical-angle analysis had been correct: the Green Mountain barrels *were* rifled with a one-in-twelve twist, just exactly as he had predicted.

32

For almost three years, it appeared to detectives, Dana had been moving money out of his grandmother's trust account, and not small amounts, either: two or three times a month, Dana as trustee for the ninety-year-old Glee Mitchell pulled amounts ranging from a thousand to as much as seven thousand dollars.

Then, in late February 1995, Dana decided to move his grandmother, herself.

It appeared that Mrs. Mitchell had suffered a broken hip the previous month; and it may have been that Dana believed she could receive better care at a nursing home, rather than the life-care facility she was accustomed to.

In any event, the investigators learned of this move of Mrs. Mitchell on February 23, when Jimmie Glee Thurmond, in Oklahoma, called the detectives to tell them that Dale had collected Mrs. Mitchell from her residence in Turlock, California, to drive her to a nursing home in Studio City, California.

Studio City was less than fifteen minutes away from the Radovcich house in the San Fernando Valley.

What was all this about? The investigators knew that Dana had been frequently dipping into Mrs. Mitchell's trust fund. Now he suddenly pulled her out of the life-care facility, where she had been living for almost a decade, and put her in a strange environment only a few minutes away from Joel Radovcich.

Was Dana planning to have Joel kill his grandmother? Was that the reason for the sudden change? Was it because Mrs. Mitchell was proving to be far more healthy and long-lived than Dana had bargained for—that Dana's raiding of Mrs. Mitchell's account would soon be exposed if she continued living at the life-care facility? Was it Dana's plan to get rid of his grandmother so he could get his hands on his share of the oil money?

It seemed that way, at least to the investigators. When detectives asked the administrators at the Turlock life-care facility what reason Dana had given for removing his grandmother, they said Dana had told them Mrs. Mitchell could no longer afford to live there.

And when the detectives called the nursing home at Studio City, they learned that Mrs. Mitchell had been assigned a room with a door that opened to the outside at Dana's insistence. Was this what Joel's electronic lock pick was to be used for—to get inside Mrs. Mitchell's room and snuff her out before she consumed too much of her own money?

No one could be sure. Already, detectives had circulated photographs of Joel at the Turlock facility, along with instructions to call the police if Joel ever turned up. Now they did the same with the Studio City nursing home; in addition, they convinced the nursing home to move Mrs. Mitchell to a more secure room, and to prevent Dana from taking his grandmother out of the facility for any reason.

33

On March 2, 1995, Sheriff Magarian, Lieutenant Wiley, Sergeant Caudle, Criminalist Boudreau, and Detective Souza had a 9 A.M. meeting with Fresno County District Attorney Ed Hunt and the supervisor of his felony murder team, Jim Oppliger. They had with them a large chart, and a briefing paper.

This time, the Sheriff's men said, they could prove their case beyond a reasonable doubt. They had hard evidence to go along with all the suspicious circumstances.

Caudill and Souza put up the chart; Caudill gave the briefing.

Laboriously, Caudill took the prosecutors over the investigation, month by month and step by step, showing everything by means of the flow chart.

One part of the chart was marked with Dana's actions, a second by Joel's, and a third by Jack Ponce's activities. Caudill also distributed a forty-eight-page briefing paper that included a fifteen-page overview of the case.

From the overview:

"Due to the length and complexity of this investigation, the following case preface is provided to assist the reader. Included in this preface [are] the opinion[s] of the investigators assigned to this case. This opinion is based upon: the physical evidence; the circumstantial evidence, the facts of the investigation; and the training, knowledge, expertise, and experience of the assigned investigators and detective management staff.

"Approximately one year prior to the Ewell family homicide, Dana Ewell and Joel Radovcich conspired to kill Dana's family. The motive for the homicides was monetary gain. Dana was aware that the family estate was valued at over seven million dollars.

"Joel Radovcich, without leaving a 'paper trail,' began obtaining the necessary tools and accessories that were used to carry out the well-planned homicides. In May, 1991, Radovcich contacted former schoolmate (Santa Clara University) Tom Duong. Radovcich asked Duong to allow Radovcich to have some books sent to Duong's residence under Duong's name (no 'paper trail'). In June, 1991, when these books arrived, Duong opened the shipping container against Radovcich's previous instructions. Duong was shocked to find the shipment contained books on how to make silencers for weapons.

"Subsequent investigation performed by Detective Souza included obtaining the shipment order form and the same materials as ordered by Radovcich and sent to the Duong residence. The silencer books gave several instructions and schematics on how to make homemade silencers. Materials necessary included steel wool and foam rubber. The manuals also gave instructions for drilling (or porting) gun barrels to further reduce the sound of the gunshot. The porting of the barrel allows gases to escape prior to the bullet exiting the gun barrel. Per the manuals ordered by Radovcich, the porting of an external barrel may be performed prior to placing a silencer over that ported barrel.

"On the cover of one of the silencer manuals was a picture of a military assault rifle with an external barrel.

"While growing up in the San Fernando Valley, Joel Radovcich and his older brother, Peter, had a very good friend in the neighborhood, Ernest "Jack" Ponce. On March 23, 1992, Jack ordered a Feather Industries AT9 9-millimeter assault rifle under Jack's name (no 'paper trail') from a gun dealer in Northridge. The weapon met the necessary specifications that allowed a silencer to be easily mounted and the external barrel ported for further sound suppression. The Feather Industries AT9 looks very similar to the assault rifle featured on the silencer book cover.

"Jack Ponce took possession of the AT9 on April 8, 1992, eleven days prior to the Ewell homicides.

"Investigators eventually learned of Jack Ponce and his relationship with Joel. During several interviews, investigators were frustrated by his nonresponsive and evasive answers and his refusal to elaborate on any question. During a third interview, Ponce reluctantly admitted that he had purchased an AT9. His reason for the purchase was to 'shoot opossums in his mothers' attic.' When asked to see [show] the weapon, Ponce related that it had been stolen from his vehicle trunk while the vehicle was parked at his girlfriend's apartment complex in a locked parking area.

"Through follow-up interviews and investigation, it was learned that Ponce was an avid shooter and would shoot often at a pistol range with Peter and Joel Radovcich. It was also learned that this avid shooter, who had several other guns, did not tell anyone that he had purchased the AT9. This included his best friend, Peter Radovcich. His girlfriend related that it would be totally out of character for Ponce to buy an assault rifle. His father indicated that the opossum story was a ridiculously untruthful excuse. A check of the LAPD vehicle burglary report indicated that it was a counter report and no one had actually observed any damage to Ponce's vehicle. Ponce had told his girlfriend and Peter Radovcich that his vehicle had been burglarized but did not tell them a gun had been taken.

"Credit card receipts show Dana traveling to the Los Angeles area in November of 1991. Dana obtained gasoline in the same San Fernando Valley neighborhood as the Radovcich residence.

"Phone tolls show pay phone contact between Dana in Santa Clara and Joel in Los Angeles on April 9, 1992 (ten days prior to the homicides). Phone toll search warrants later revealed contact between Dana and Joel, after the homicides, on these same phones. This has been determined through surveillance, search warrants, and investigation conducted by detectives that has established a pattern of pager utilization and the use of pay phones to maintain communication between Joel and Dana, as set for hereinafter.

"On April 18, 1992, the Ewell family departed company [sic] from their Pajaro Dunes beach house. Dana returned to the Morgan Hill and Santa Clara area setting up a 'paper trail' alibi as he traveled. This was accomplished by retaining cash register receipts for Easter cards and using a credit card to purchase a small amount of groceries. It is believed that the suspect or suspects were already in the Ewells' Sunnyside home and were lying in wait after ransacking the residence in a staged and faked burglary.

"The burglary appeared obviously staged to the team of homicide investigators assigned to the investigation. Every drawer was pulled out but sometimes in the wrong order (top to bottom) rather than bottom to top as a professional burglar does. Bed sheets were laid out to carry property, rather than pillow cases. Stereo equipment wires were carefully unscrewed rather than quickly pulled out. Miscellaneous coins and music cassettes (of no value) were placed on the sheets.

"When homicide investigators were ready to release the residence back to Dana Ewell, they first summoned burglary investigators to the scene. Without prompting, homicide investigators asked each burglary investigator to view the residence. Each burglary investigator, on his own, viewed the residence and then related that the burglary appeared strange to them. Those investigators felt that the burglary was staged and questioned the lack of any sign of forced entry into the residence.

"Investigators believe that during the ransacking of the residence, the suspect went to the master bedroom and obtained the family Browning 9-millimeter pistol and old Winchester 9-millimeter ammunition from a nightstand where he knew they would be. The suspect then opened the box of ammunition and took some rounds from the box, placing those rounds in the AT9 that he brought with him. The suspect later took the Browning pistol from the residence. He also left the ammunition box opened in obvious plain sight in a displayed fashion.

"This ingenious plan, believed developed by Dana and Radovcich, was intended to lead investigators to believe that burglar(s) had broken into the Ewell residence and ransacked it, locating the family Browning 9-millimeter and 9-millimeter ammunition. When the burglar was surprised by the family returning home, he shot each family member and fled the residence with the 9-millimeter. Dana reported that the only property missing was the 9-millimeter and a string of pearls. However, the plan was not as foolproof as Dana and Joel believed it was.

"When bullets were recovered at the crime scene, Supervising Criminalist Allen Boudreau of the Sheriff's Department Crime Lab observed very unusual markings on the bullets. The bullets were actually etched with unusual linear striations that were consistent with each fired bullet. This indicated that the bullets were all fired by the same gun but something marked the bullets as they traveled down the barrel. Boudreau believed the firearm firing the bullets was altered in some fashion, possibly by a silencer.

"In a check with numerous other recognized firearms examiners, it was agreed that the bullets were extremely unusual and did not appear to come from any known firearm, unless that firearm had been altered.

"The murder bullets were then sent, along with the Winchester ammunition from the residence, to the FBI Crime Lab in Washington, D.C., for elemental analysis. The analysis proved that the murder bullets came from the same lot as the 1971 ammunition in the Ewell residence. A sales receipt located by investigators showed the purchase of the Browning 9-millimeter and the 9-millimeter ammunition by Dale Ewell in 1971.

"An examination of the murder bullets indicated the same direction of twist and number of lands and grooves as a Browning 9-millimeter pistol. However, the rate of twist (not commonly referred to by lay people) did not match the Browning. A check with the Browning Company confirmed that there was absolutely no way that a Browning 9-millimeter pistol could have fired the murder bullets.

"This scientific fact left investigators with the knowledge that the killer(s) had entered the residence with a somehow altered 9-millimeter weapon knowing that there was a 9-millimeter Browning and ammunition in the master bedroom. The killer(s) took the old Winchester ammunition from the box in the bedroom and loaded the bullets into their weapon. The killer(s) shot and killed the Ewell family with the altered 9-millimeter and took the Browning from the residence. The killer(s) picked up the ejected casings and took them from the residence, knowing that the ejector marks would not match to a Browning 9-millimeter pistol.

"The linear striations were extremely unusual and unless bullets had been shot and recovered, the shooter would not know that the bullets would be so unusually marked. This unusual marking even stumped the aforementioned firearms experts. The cause of the markings was finally determined to be caused by drilling (or porting) the gun barrel as per Radovcich's weapons books. When Allen Boudreau followed the book's directions in a scientific reproduction, he replicated the markings in a remarkably similar fashion. Investigators obtained an AT9 of the same generation as Ponce's gun. The gun was ported per the book. The fired bullets looked exactly like those fired from the murder weapon. No other means have been located that will replicate the unusual markings.

"Trace evidence was collected at the scene that later proved to be unusual. The trace evidence consisted of minute particles of steel wool and foam rubber. When performing reproduction tests, per Joel's gun book, Allen Boudreau also built a silencer per book instructions. The silencer was placed over the ported barrel, per book instructions. When Boudreau fired the weapon, he found that the escaping gasses from the ported holes would blow minute particles of steel wool and foam rubber through the AT9 vented heat shroud silencer. These particles would then fall in front of the shooter. Those particles are exactly like those found around the murdered Ewell family members.

"Investigators then felt that it was very likely that the Ponce AT9 was the murder weapon. Subsequent investigation confirmed their opinions. Upon contacting Feather Industries, it was learned that the barrels were manufactured by Green Mountain Barrel Company of New Hampshire. Investigators traveled to both companies and learned that Ponce's weapon was of a limited generation of AT9s that were fitted with a barrel that had been rifled with a rate of twist of a complete turn in twelve [inches]. The rate of twist places the speed of spin on a bullet and scientific examinations of fired bullets can determine the rate of twist. The industry standard is a turn in ten [inches].

"Investigators also contacted gun owners that [sic] had purchased AT9s of the same generation as Ponce's weapon (Serial #A92407) with the turn-in-twelve [inch] barrel. Investigators obtained barrels from Serial #A92406 and #A92395 for testing. Barrel #A92406 was placed on an AT9 and ported exactly to the specifications of Joel's book. The fired bullets exactly matched each scientific characteristic as the murder bullets. (Lands and grooves, rate of twist, and extremely unusual markings.) Nothing else will replicate these exact characteristics.

"Investigators then contacted and contracted [with] world-renowned firearms experts Lucien Haag. Haag is an expert for such companies as Winchester Western. He is commonly used as a defense expert in civil lawsuits and as a prosecution expert for major law enforcement agencies.

"Haag was asked to review numerous scientific examinations to confirm, or deny [refute], the tests and reproductions performed by the FSO Crime Lab (Boudreau). Haag's conclusions completely supported Boudreau's scientific conclusions.

"After the homicides, surviving Ewell family members (uncles and aunts) noticed that Dana was acting in a very unusual manner. He showed little or no concern for his slain family members. However, he did show a great deal of concern over how much money he would actually receive and when he would receive it.

"When the family residence (crime scene) was turned back over to Dana, investigators observed Dana's behavior to be unusual. Dana was taken on a 'walk-through' of the residence by investigators. This is a common practice of returning control of a crime scene back over to family members. During this 'walk-through,' Dana showed no emotion when walking around obvious bloodstains left by his dead father, mother, and sister. However, he did get angry at FSO personnel for accidentally clipping a hall light fixture wire when obtaining evidence. Dana did not inquire about his safety in the residence or how the investigation was progressing. Dana did demand an inventory list of everything taken from the residence.

"When going through the backyard, Dana quickly grabbed a key from a hiding spot in an outdoor shed when he felt the investigators were not looking. He then quickly thrust the key in his pocket. Investigators had not known of the key's existence prior to Dana's unusual actions. Investigators were unable to locate any sign of forced entry into the residence.

"Dana's participation, and cooperation, with investigating officers was, at best, minimal. When inquiries were made regarding his old friend Joel Radovcich, Dana's cooperation dropped to nonexistent. Dana refused to discuss Radovcich with investigators. Dana ran from FSO headquarters when asked to talk about Radovcich. When Dana was told by investigators that they felt Radovcich was responsible for the Ewell murders, he arrogantly refused to discuss the matter, stating 'this isn't the proper time.' Immediately after investigators left, Dana and Monica Zent were observed leaving Dana's dorm and driving away utilizing countersurveillance-type driving skills that forced surveillance officers off the surveillance. Then minutes later Joel was paged in southern California to call a pay phone in Santa Clara. Surveillance officers then drove to the pay phone in Santa Clara which was located in a deserted commercial parking complex. As investigators entered the complex, they observed Dana and Monica driving out.

"Dana has continued his relationship with Joel. Dana and Joel flew to Mexico together in Dana's airplane and then flew back together to the Fresno Air Terminal. When surveillance officers began to follow the pair in a vehicle from the airport, Dana exited the vehicle and ran toward the undercover surveillance vehicle.

"Investigation and surveillance revealed a very close relationship between Dana and Joel. This relationship existed prior to, and after, the homicides. Dana has paid over $7,000 for numerous types of flight lessons for Joel. Financial search warrants show that Dana had withdrawn $74,105 from bank accounts between May of '92 and July of '93. The investigation has also documented numerous clandestine phone calls between the two. Sixty-seven phone calls and pages are documented at this time. Overheard phone conversations indicate Dana and Joel feel they could be arrested but view the crime as a game that they are smart enough to win.

"During surveillance, contact was observed between Radovcich and Ponce (five documented calls and pages and a personal clandestine contact) at the same period of time as numerous clandestine contacts between Radovcich and Dana.

"Prior to the homicides, both Dana and Joel bragged to friends that they would be millionaires by age twenty-five. They are the same age. Dana mistakenly believed that he would inherit the entire estate at age twenty-five should Dale, Glee, and Tiffany all die leaving him as the sole inheritor. According to his parents, Joel has never been employed and has no visible source of income. Investigators believe that the conspiracy included Dana paying Joel at least one million dollars for the execution of Dana's family when Dana received the inheritance at twenty-five.

"During interviews with Ponce, he was extremely vague

and untruthful. His reason for the purchase of the AT9, and his failure to tell anyone about the exotic firearm, is both questionable and unreasonable. The reported theft of the firearm, without documented physical evidence to support a vehicle burglary, occurred conveniently after investigators had interviewed Joel Radovcich. The firearm has never been recovered.

"Jack Ponce's father indicated to investigators that his son's appearance changed dramatically after the investigators' first interview with Jack. This healthy young man suddenly lost twenty-five pounds and was reported to be very depressed. When questioned by his father regarding this serious weight loss, Jack related that he believed Joel was involved in a 'Menendez Brothers'-type homicide.

"It is believed by investigators that two very bright young men planned and executed what they felt would be the perfect crime. Both young men wanted wealth but neither wanted to toil for that wealth. Dana's wealthy family provided Dana with the opportunity to easily, and quickly, obtain that wealth. The execution of his family was merely a necessity. Joel's brilliant mind, but strange and antisocial personality and behavior, provided the perfect planner and executioner.

"When these suspects were surprised by the thorough and exhaustive investigation conducted by the Sheriff's detectives, the suspects continued communications in a clandestine fashion they felt was too clever for the investigators to discover. The three suspects' actions, behavior, and refusal to assist in this brutal homicide investigation, that they claim no knowledge of, only betrays their claim of innocence."

Now was the time to strike, said Magarian. With this evidence, the detectives had a window of opportunity to get Jack Ponce to turn state's witness against Joel and Dana.

Hunt and Oppliger were convinced. The ballistics evidence seemed irrefutable.

"Pick 'em up," said Hunt.

END
GAME

34

The afternoon of that same day, two surveillance teams reached Southern California. One team set up on Joel's mother's house, waiting for him to show up there. The other tracked Jack to his job at the Ontario restaurant.

A third surveillance team set up on the Ewell house to watch Dana. That team saw Dana leave the house in his Mercedes, but they lost him.

When Joel showed up in the neighborhood of his mother's house, the surveilling officers could hardly believe their eyes. Joel had attempted to peroxide his hair blond; the results instead made it look orange. But having a bad-hair day was the least of Joel's problems. Ernie Burk put Joel under arrest. Joel said nothing as the surveillance team booked him in Los Angeles, then made arrangements to take him to Fresno the following day.

Meanwhile, the team following Jack surrounded the Ontario restaurant, and then telephoned Fresno. Souza, Caudill, Curtice, and Oppliger flew down to Ontario in a private plane to make the pinch.

Jack was at his station behind the bar when the four went into the restaurant. To avoid a scene, Caudill asked the restaurant manager to summon Jack to a back room. There he was placed under arrest for murder, exactly as Souza had predicted nearly a year before. Jack was taken from the restaurant and booked into jail in San Bernardino.

Like Joel, Jack at first said little, asking only that he be allowed to talk to a lawyer. But the following day, Jack talked to his father, Dr. Ernest Ponce. Late Friday afternoon, Jack was driven to Fresno in a two-car caravan. Little was said. Souza suggested that Jack cooperate, that things might go easier on him if he did.

After booking at the Fresno County Jail, Jack talked briefly to a lawyer. Later the same night he was interviewed by the investigators.

And where was Dana? His surveillance team returned to the Ewell house in the anticipation that Dana would sooner or later return, but as the afternoon turned into the evening, he still didn't show. Had Dana somehow gotten word of the arrest warrants? Had he made a break for it? No one could be sure.

It was as if Dana had simply disappeared.

35

"I'll tell you what you want to know," Jack Ponce told the two detectives. Sergeant Caudill and Detective Curtice turned on their tape recorder.

After a night in jail, thinking about the gas chamber, Jack was standing on the precipice. For almost three years he had kept the secrets. Now he faced a realistic prospect of spending the rest of his still-young life in a prison cell, if not being executed. His father's words weighed heavily on his mind.

"I hate to see you waste your life," Dr. Ponce had told his son earlier that day. "If you know anything about this, you'd better tell them."

When he thought about his father, Jack felt like crying. It hadn't always been easy for the two of them, over the years. But now that he was in the worst trouble he'd even been in, his father was standing behind him, still caring for him. Dr. Ponce had helped arrange for Curtis Sisk to represent Jack. Sisk met with the police and the District Attorney's office, and a deal had been struck: if Jack answered the detectives' questions truthfully, he might receive favorable treatment. Otherwise, he would fall into the abyss with Joel and Dana Ewell. Strange, Jack thought: all this was about this Dana Ewell person, whom he'd never even met.

It had begun, Jack told the detectives, in March 1992. He'd been living with his girlfriend. His father had cut him off, no more money, and Jack was broke. That was when Joel had asked him to buy the gun.

"He asked me, 'What do you need for it?' " Jack said. "I told him I only needed five hundred."

There wasn't any doubt about what Joel was up to, Jack told the detectives. Joel had made it clear he wanted to keep his own name off any gun purchase. Given all of Joel's experiments with silencers during the previous summer, Jack was certain that Joel was going to make a silencer for the new gun. Then, Jack believed, Joel intended to sell the silenced AT9 at a premium on the black market. All Jack would have to do is buy the gun, and then report it stolen.

When had Joel first begun the experiments with the silencers? the investigators wanted to know.

The summer before that, Jack told them. Jack told how he had given Joel a .380 automatic pistol, and how the two of them had gone to the gun show and bought the barrel extension for the pistol. Peter had welded the pipe on the .380. The first silencer didn't work that well, Jack said. Later the same summer he'd given Joel a .22 Beretta, and Joel had made a silencer for that, too. It looked like a Coke can, Joel said, and was filled with circles of rubber cut from tennis balls.

After that summer, Joel had returned to Santa Clara University, while Jack moved back into his Santa Monica apartment to attend classes at UCLA. He'd had a little contact with Joel that fall, but not much.

The following March, though, Joel had called Jack at Jack's girlfriend's apartment and asked him to buy the AT9. Joel told Jack he'd pay him extra to buy the gun; since Jack wanted to buy a used van from Peter's plumbing shop and didn't have the money for it, he'd agreed to the deal.

Later, though, he'd talked with Peter. Jack had asked Peter why he didn't buy the gun for Joel. "He said he didn't want to," Jack said.

On March 23, 1992, Joel gave Jack $1,500 in hundred-dollar bills. Jack went to the gun dealer in Northridge and ordered the AT9. Joel had asked Jack to get some subsonic ammunition as well—the sort of ammunition that made a silencer work better, since the velocity of the bullet was below the sound barrier.

The salesperson at the store wouldn't sell the subsonic rounds, Jack said.

"He just looked at me for a minute and then said, 'We don't have that,'" Jack said. Jack wrote a check for the AT9, then went to the bank to deposit $1,000 of Joel's $1,500. Next he went to Peter's plumbing shop to buy the van. It wasn't a very good bargain: for involving himself in a triple murder, he'd gotten a used van. Not only that, the transmission and the tires were bad.

On April 8, Jack continued, he'd picked up the AT9, and drove immediately over to Peter's apartment, where he'd given the rifle to Joel. He'd already returned the remainder of Joel's money from the $1,500.

Later, Joel had called him at Jack's girlfriend's apartment, Jack said. Joel wanted him to come over to the Radovcich family garage to see something.

Joel was acting very secretive. He took Jack into the garage and locked the door. Next he pulled down a backpack from a shelf. He withdrew the AT9 from the backpack. Jack saw that it had been modified with a thick black tube around the barrel. Joel assembled the weapon.

"Watch this," Joel said, and he fired the gun two or three times into a log. The silencer worked.

Did the gun make any sound?

"Like a pop," Jack told the detectives.

"Immediately after you gave the gun to him, was it—how long did it take him to—"

"It was—it was awhile."

"Months, or—"

"Well, maybe not that long. Maybe about a week. It really wasn't that long. He was working on it, working on it, suddenly it was okay."

"Were you over at the house quite a bit when he was doing that, building the silencer?"

"Yeah," Jack said.

After the murders, Jack said, he and Peter got rid of a lot of stuff that Joel wanted them to lose.

Caudill and Curtice asked Jack, What sort of stuff?

PVC pipe. It was black.

"Black PVC pipe?"

"Yeah."

"What other materials did you see?"

"Tennis balls."

"How were the tennis balls used?"

"He was cutting them in circles."

"Cutting a circle on them?"

"Yeah, cutting them in a circle for something, a baffle."

Well, where did Joel get this equipment, to build this silencer?

"We went down to Pete's house [actually, Joel's mother's house] and we opened up the garage. I think he was, well, I saw the thing in the garage at his mom's house."

"Okay."

"So he was machining on it and working on it."

Then the day had come when the silencer was ready, and Joel invited Jack over to see the test shots into the log.

"You're going to sell that, make a lot of money?" Jack asked Joel.

"Yeah," Joel said.

All right, said Caudle and Curtice. Tell us when you first heard about the murders.

"When Joel told me and when you guys told me," Jack said. "And look[ing] it up in the newspaper when the article comes out."

Well, of course, this wasn't exactly true, since the Los Angeles area newspapers hadn't carried the story about the murders, and Jack hadn't even been contacted by the Sheriff's detectives until October of 1993.

So Joel told you about the murders? the detectives asked.
Yes, said Jack.

How did he get into the house? Did he tell you that?

"Through the window of the garage."

"Okay. So you don't know if he had a key or not?"

"No, no key."

Did he say anything about alarms?

"No, nothing about an alarm, just something about the back window, the back window, the garage window, something like that."

"Was the family there when he got there?"

"No," said Jack, "I believe he got there before them and waited."

Joel told him, Jack told the detectives, that "it was getting light" when he shot the Ewells, and that he'd had to wait the entire day in the house, with the dead victims, until it got dark enough to be safe for him to leave.

This, of course, wasn't true, since the detectives already knew that the Ewells had been shot soon after their late afternoon arrival. But whether this was a misunderstanding on Jack's part, or dramatic embroidery by Joel wasn't clear. Souza wasn't sure whether Joel was lying to Jack, or if Jack had simply gotten the story garbled. He was later to say, however, that he didn't believe everything Jack said Joel had said, an assertion that would come back to haunt him later.

"Where was Joel waiting?" the detectives asked.

Jack had a rudimentary understanding of the layout of the Ewell house.

"The hallway goes—you walk this way and there's a door here, and a perpendicular kind of door from where the hallway is," said Jack, providing a recognizable description of the corridor between the garages and the kitchen.

Did Joel take anything from the house?

Joel told him that he'd taken a gun, Jack told the detectives. Joel said he'd taken the pistol to cover his tracks.

What was Joel's source of money? the detectives asked.

Joel, Jack said, had access to Dana's bank account

through a bank teller card. Joel was angry at Dana, Jack told the detectives, because Joel thought Dana was spending too much money on Monica Zent.

Joel told him what had happened at the Ewell house when both were staying at Jack's girlfriend's apartment after the murders. He remembered when, he said, because it happened during the Rodney King riots.

It was during the riots, Jack said, that Joel had told him the details of the murders—including Joel's attempts to feel the pulses of the victims, and Joel's worry that somehow the victims had survived.

"I said," Jack told the detectives, " 'Well, you know, if you're not there, maybe they're good actors, because there's no way anybody could sit still that long and be hurt that bad.' "

At some point in this long first interview, either Caudill or Curtice popped the most important question of all: Did Jack know where the gun was now?

Most of it, Jack said, had been thrown away. But, Jack said, he knew where parts of it were—"important parts."

Like what?

Like the barrel, Jack said.

The word went up the chain of command, from Caudill to Wiley to the captain, then to the undersheriff, who came to see Sheriff Magarian.

He says he knows where the barrel is, the undersheriff told Magarian.

"Thank God," said Magarian. Then another thought struck. "Let's pray it's still there."

On the Monday following the arrests, Dana and Joel spent Day One of their new lives. Gone were the Mercedes, the Honda, the expensive restaurants, the trips to Mexico, the flying lessons, the new airplane; gone as well were the designer clothes and shoes.

Instead of Armani and Gucci, both Joel and Dana, shackled by hands and feet, were dressed in maroon Fresno County Jail jumpsuits and plastic sandals. This would be their daily attire for the next two years, and there wasn't a thing either Dana or Joel could do about it.

Detective Curtice was there to watch. Like the other detectives, he'd taken offense long before at Dana's seeming condescending attitude.

"I wanted to see," Curtice said, "if he'd have a Polo pony on his jumpsuit."

But this was only the start of some powerful changes in the Ewell family. In fact, the arrests had set off what appeared to be a mad scramble among the Ewell and Irvin survivors for the control of the money.

Someone else went to court on that same Monday, too—Michael Dowling. The executor of the Ewell estate wanted court to order all of Dana's accounts frozen.

This was bad news for Dana—very bad news. He'd previously paid $250,000 to Berman for his representation.

The news of the arrests broke across Fresno like the shock wave from a long anticipated but still uncertain explosion.

EWELL ARREST MADE, headlined the *Bee* on Saturday, March 4.

Former College Roommate Held in Breakthrough in Three-Year-Old Case; Sheriff's Officials Also Issue Warrant for Son's Arrest in Slayings of Family

"A former college classmate of Dana Ewell has been arrested for the 1992 shooting deaths of Ewell's family," wrote *Bee* reporter Royal Calkins, "and Fresno County sheriff's officials this morning issued an all-points bulletin for the arrest of Ewell.

"Sheriff's deputies spent Friday night looking for Ewell and searching the scene of the triple slaying, the family's home on East Park Circle Drive in Fresno's Sunnyside neighborhood."

No one would say what the investigators were looking for in the Ewell house, Calkins reported, noting that the house had already been thoroughly searched in the days following the murders.

Calkins described Joel as a roommate of Dana's at Santa Clara, which was something of an overstatement, since the two never had actually roomed together. Joel's lawyer, Woolf, said he had talked to Joel on Friday afternoon—

nearly a day after the arrest. Joel, Woolf told the *Bee*, "denies any involvement."

And Calkins added:

"Sheriff's detectives late Friday also were reportedly questioning another Southern California man who was suspected of supplying the weapon to Radovcich."

That same Saturday, while Dana Ewell was still among the missing, Jack was back in the San Fernando Valley, very close, in fact, to Peter's old apartment building.

Jack directed the detectives accompanying him to an alley near the apartment. He recalled the events of the night that he and Peter had thrown away the contents of the backpack, leaving Jack with just the gun barrel.

Peter had run up the stairs to see what was the matter with Danielle, Jack recalled. I didn't go. Instead I walked down this alley for a couple of blocks.

The investigators accompanying Jack followed him down the alley.

I came to this empty field, Jack said. That one, with the rickety fence.

Jack and the investigators came to the field and the fence.

I found a place to go over the fence, Jack said, right about here. Jack pointed to a place where it was easier to scale the fence.

Jack and the investigators went into the field.

This is where I buried it, Jack said, pointing to a spot not too far from the fence.

The investigators began digging. Within a few minutes they struck metal.

It was a gun barrel, all right. About eighteen inches long, rusted, of course. But along the sides one could still plainly see the line of holes someone had drilled into it to make it a murderously silent engine of destruction.

Dana was in San Diego when he got the word from his lawyer, Richard Berman: he was wanted for murder, and an all-points bulletin was out for his arrest—a bulletin

which described Dana as dangerous and p with a 9-millimeter assault rifle.

Berman was in Long Beach attending a Bar meeting when he heard about the warrants—a points bulletin. He was peeved at the Sheriff's De earlier, he'd assured that if and when the detective to arrest Dana, he'd make arrangements for Dana himself in, so there would be no question that he w a fugitive.

That hadn't happened; police had given no warning, now Dana couldn't be located. It was all so unnecessa Berman thought, and even a bit underhanded, especially th part that suggested Dana was some sort of heavily arme desperado.

Whether Dana called Berman, or Berman called Dana wasn't immediately clear. Or, possibly, someone else who knew about the warrants and the bulletin called Dana on Saturday, the day of the first *Bee* story, to let him know what was happening. In any event, that afternoon, Dana called Berman to ask him what to do. Berman advised Dana to drive to Long Beach, where they would both go to the Long Beach Police Department to turn Dana in. Berman didn't want to take any chances some trigger-happy cop would blow the "armed and dangerous" Dana away.

Just before 9 P.M., Dana and Berman walked into Long Beach Police Department headquarters, where Dana turne himself in. Berman lost little time airing his gripe with th police.

"I had told the Sheriff's Department repeatedly throu out this investigation that if they wanted him, all they to do was call and he would surrender. He was nev fugitive. The second he learned he was wanted, we arrangements to turn him in."

The following afternoon, Dana was transpor Fresno. As he walked, shackled, into the jail, a large of news reporters besieged him with questions.

"Were you involved in the murder of your fan

"Absolutely not," Dana said, visibly angry. " way. This is ridiculous."

Now Dowling wanted the court to order Berman to repay the money to the estate. Without being able to pay Berman, Dana would have to be defended by a lawyer from the Public Defender's Office. This was about as far as a Gucci/Polo-wearing, Mercedes-driving, high-flyer could sink: having to be defended by the low-paid, overworked, government-appointed defenders of the criminal poor.

Meanwhile, Dana's uncles were also rushing into court. Within a few days of the arrests, they hired a lawyer, Russell Georgeson, to seek a temporary restraining order against Dowling to forbid him to distribute any more funds from the estate to Dana.

If Dana were convicted of murder, then half of the Ewell estate would go first, to the estate of Austin Ewell, Sr.—Dale's father. But since Austin had died in the summer of 1994, that meant his estate—and with it, the rights to Dale's estate—would go to his surviving children, Dale's sister Betty Whitted, and the three surviving brothers—Richard, Dan, and Ben, Jr. The other half, or Glee Ewell's portion, would go to Glee Mitchell—Dana's grandmother, who was still in the nursing home in Studio City.

Dan Ewell filed a complaint in the probate court that accused Dana of causing the murders, and a second legal action to prevent Dana from inheriting about $140,000 from a trust from the estate of Glee Mitchell's deceased husband, James J. Mitchell; Dan Ewell was one of the trustees of that estate. One thing was clear: the brothers of Dale Ewell weren't about to let a dime of either side of the family's money go to defend Dana, if they could help it.

Dana's lawyer, Berman, wasted no time in pointing the finger of greed at Dana's uncles.

"This is a shameless attempt to deny Dana the funds he needs to prove his innocence," Berman said. The uncles' motives were clear, he added: they wanted their brother's money for themselves.

"Dana doesn't want the money for a vacation in Hawaii," Berman continued. "It's to prove his innocence, to spare himself the gas chamber, which is where his greedy uncles would prefer to see him go, so *they* can go to Hawaii.''

Georgeson fired back on behalf of the brothers.

''Mr. Berman is sadly mistaken in his allegations, period,'' he said.

Amidst all this family feuding, Jimmie Glee Thurmond and her mother came to town to see what could be done about moving Glee Mitchell back to Oklahoma—only to discover that Dana had very nearly exhausted the cash reserves of Glee Mitchell's life-care estate.

Once in Fresno, Jimmie Glee and Mrs. Sargent were put in contact with a lawyer who was a friend of Glee Ewell, Ruth Lind. Ruth Lind asked to be appointed conservator of Mrs. Mitchell's trust in place of Dana. Jimmie Glee Thurmond and her mother signed the papers approving this appointment, reasoning that Ruth Lind would help them get custody of Mrs. Mitchell so she could go back to her family in Oklahoma. It was only later that Jimmie Glee and Mrs. Sargent realized that Ruth Lind would not allow Mrs. Mitchell to go back to Oklahoma.

Instead, she wanted Mrs. Mitchell to be returned to the life-care facility in Turlock, and argued in court that removal to Oklahoma at this stage might be injurious or even fatal to her health. Jimmie Glee and Mrs. Sargent believed Lind thought they only wanted custody of Mrs. Mitchell for her money.

Mrs. Thurmond and Mrs. Sargent later claimed, on the contrary, it was Ms. Lind who wanted Mrs. Mitchell's money, and they suggested that Lind would do whatever was necessary to keep control of Mrs. Mitchell's estate, so she could keep earning her fees as conservator of the estate. They said they wished they'd never agreed to Ruth Lind's appointment as Mrs. Mitchell's conservator. In the end, the court agreed with Ms. Lind. Mrs. Mitchell stayed in California.

And as if all this weren't enough, about a week after the arrest, Dana's aunt, Betty Whitted back in Ohio, announced she would forego her quarter-share of the half of the Ewell estate so that Dana could have money to defend himself. She would turn over her share of Austin Sr.'s estate to Dana so he could defend himself.

Furious, the three brothers turned on their sister. Five days later, Mrs. Whitted reversed herself, and said she wouldn't make the money available after all. Then two days later, a lawyer for Mrs. Whitted said she was "unequivocally in favor" of turning the money over to Dana.

Richard, Dan, and Ben rushed back to Ohio to prevent their sister from using any of the money in Austin Sr.'s estate to help Dana pay for a lawyer. On April 6, 1995, the three brothers obtained a temporary restraining order in an Ohio court that prevented Betty Whitted from using any of Austin Sr.'s funds for Dana's defense.

They were, said Dana's uncles, only following the expressed wishes of the patriarch, Austin Sr. His will, they said, contained the following clause:

"I deliberately make no provision for Dana Ewell." Austin had gone to his death in the generator explosion believing that his grandson had caused the murder of his son, and for reasons of pure greed.

38

In the week following the arrests of Joel, Jack, and Dana, and based on the statements of Jack, the detectives returned to Southern California, not only to look over the areas where Jack claimed he and Peter had dumped evidence, but also to arrest Peter, based on Jack's account of what happened the night the contents of the backpack were thrown out.

In interviewing Peter, the detectives soon learned that Peter had been well aware that Joel had made a silencer—in fact, Peter admitted, he'd helped Joel by welding a washer on a gun barrel. But, Peter said, he'd had no idea of what Joel intended to do with the modified gun. It was only after Joel had come to him in a panic, Peter said, that he realized Joel was involved in very bad business.

Based on his own admissions—welding the washer on the barrel as the support for the silencer, and later, disposing of the evidence—Peter was also liable for criminal charges. But on balance, Peter seemed to be the least involved. A bargain was struck: in return for his truthful testimony, Peter would not be charged for his part in the murders. After giving a lengthy statement to the detectives, Peter said he still wasn't convinced his brother had actually pulled the trigger. It was too hard to believe, he said.

*   *   *

By the middle of March 1995, a number of details of the Sheriff's Department investigation of Dana had begun to emerge publicly.

Reporters for the *Bee* gained access to portions of the affidavits in support of the search warrants written by Souza. Later, there was confusion over how the newspaper obtained the portions, or whether, even, any single affidavit was complete. It appeared that the affidavits had been filed with the court at the time the warrants were issued in 1992, 1993, and 1994, then sealed by the issuing judge, Lawrence O'Neill.

But with the arrests, it also appeared that for a few days at least some parts of the affidavits had been circulated to the newspaper. When prosecutors read the details of these affidavits in the *Bee*, they rushed back to Judge O'Neill for an order resealing them. The newspaper then filed a court action to force O'Neill to unseal all the affidavits.

In the meantime, however, the *Bee*'s reporters had access to some portions of nearly seventy pages of affidavits, mostly written by Souza, in which a number of phrases attributed to Joel in the putative conversations with Dana were included.

From the defense perspective, the problem with the leakage was its very selectivity. Rather than reporting all of the information—including whatever evidence of reliability of the information had been used by the detectives—the newspaper was being used to show that Dana and Joel were very possibly guilty.

And also as a result, people in Fresno read for the first time that detectives had been following Joel, and that Joel had made a number of telephone calls to someone believed to be Dana, and that the gun that might have been used in the murders appeared to have been supplied to Joel by Jack Ponce. The gun, the newspaper reported, matched the ballistic characteristics of the bullets used to murder the Ewell family.

Three days after reporting the contents of some of the affidavits, the newspaper scored another coup:

DETECTIVES SEEKING DANA EWELL'S GIRLFRIEND, the *Bee* reported.

"Fresno County Sheriff's detectives investigating the Ewell murders traveled to San Diego this week to question Dana Ewell's girlfriend about money she received after the 1992 triple slaying," said the *Bee*.

The paper also reported that lawyers representing Dowling, acting for the estate, had been trying to locate Monica Zent to serve her with a restraining order forbidding her to dispose of any property or money that might have been provided to her by Dana. John Zent of the FBI had received a similar court order, the *Bee* said.

"Sheriff's officials," the *Bee* continued, "said Ewell may have bought Monica Zent a new car and paid for her living expenses in San Diego. They also believe he paid her tuition at the University of San Diego Law School."

"This case revolves around dollars," the paper quoted an unnamed Sheriff's official as saying—a suggestion that Monica Zent may have profited from her association with Dana, and his alibi. Eventually the court orders involving the Zents were rendered moot when lawyers representing the Ewell estate agreed to replenish Mrs. Mitchell's accounts to make up for the money Dana had removed.

Still, it was now clear to the defense lawyers, Berman and Woolf, that the newspaper had a pipeline into Magarian's department. The revelations contained in the search affidavits, first selective in their use by Souza and the other detectives, then doubly selective by the newspaper, seemed to the defense a calculated effort to poison the atmosphere against Dana and Joel. Parts of the affidavits, in fact, seemed to suggest that Dana and Joel were homosexual lovers, an assertion that was vociferously attacked as untrue and a form of character assassination of the two defendants, their lawyers told the *Bee*.

Now there was the new story: that Dana's girlfriend, Monica, may have somehow gained by her association with Dana.

If this publicity kept up, Berman and Woolf reasoned, it

was going to be impossible to obtain a fair trial in Fresno County. But there was more to come.

On Sunday, April 16, the *Bee* broke a new story:

WAS EWELL'S GRANDMOTHER NEXT TARGET? RELATIVES OF GLEE MITCHELL SAY DETECTIVES EXPRESSED CONCERN ABOUT HER SAFETY, the newspaper headlined on page 1.

After reporting that investigators had warned two nursing homes taking care of Glee Mitchell to take special precautions to prevent her from being murdered, the paper recounted Dana's decision to move Mrs. Mitchell to the Studio City facility, along with the speculation about the electronic lock pick and Joel.

Berman said the detectives' suspicions about Dana's intentions toward his grandmother were "utter nonsense.

"I know the reasons that she was moved to the Los Angeles area and they are very sound and reasonable. This is just another attempt at character assassination in the court of public opinion, because they don't have any evidence to convict Dana in a court of law," Berman said.

The reason Dana moved Mrs. Mitchell, Berman said, was that it was easier for Dana to visit her in Studio City than in Turlock—because it was on the way to San Diego, where Dana often visited Monica Zent.

"It sounds like they're grasping at straws," Joel's lawyer, Woolf, agreed.

Late in March, the *Bee*'s attempts to get the complete search and arrest warrant affidavits—in effect, the body of facts behind the detectives' suspicions—was rebuffed by Judge O'Neill, when defense lawyers Berman and Woolf objected, and were supported by the District Attorney's office, although for entirely different reasons.

The affidavits, Woolf and Berman asserted, were so poorly written and so rife with unsupported speculation and blind assertions that they might as well be considered junk justice. Allowing this unvalidated material out into the court of public opinion would be manifestly unfair to the accused.

"The affidavits in support of the search warrants and arrest warrants are essentially identical," Woolf said. "The first fifteen pages contain a preface which in many portions reads like a 'B' grade novel, including gratuitously insulting language. The remaining pages of the affidavits contain some factual information, which unfortunately is interwoven with unsupported conclusions, irrelevant comments, and portions of telephone conversations allegedly overheard by law enforcement officers.

"The officers submitting the affidavits put the most negative 'spin' on those portions of conversations they were able to overhear, and the press can be expected to do the same. The court is asked to take judicial notice of the press coverage thus far during the case, including front-page stories in the *Fresno Bee* nearly every day since the arrest of the defendants, along with almost daily coverage on every radio and television station in the area. There does not appear to have been a criminal case in Fresno that has generated this kind of unrelenting publicity."

Berman was even more critical of the Sheriff's Department's work.

"An affidavit of this type, under California law, is supposed to contain a statement of facts from which a neutral and detached magistrate can determine if the underlying probable cause exists," Berman said.

"The documents in question do not contain facts, but rather contain innuendo, rumor, opinions, speculation, and character assassination. In fact, these affidavits are so far removed from that which is normally and properly found in a criminal proceeding that they most closely resemble a supermarket tabloid story or a cheap novella.

"Dana Ewell is not talking about suppression of evidence or excluding evidence," Berman continued, "he is attempting to avoid the dissemination of 'non-evidence.' "

The non-evidence, Berman said, included so much rumor and speculation that the detectives had engaged in "quantum leaps" of the imagination.

"The sole intent," Berman concluded, "is to tell a fairy

tale so as to prejudice Dana Ewell and further a campaign of character assassination and a prosecution which has not to date produced any evidence as to Dana Ewell's involvement in these alleged crimes.''

The District Attorney's objections to release of the affidavits were different, Oppliger said. The case was still under investigation, he said, and unsealing the affidavits might jeopardize any new information that might be developed.

The court agreed with both the prosecution and the defense that the affidavits should remained sealed.

"I will state," said Judge O'Neill, "that there are intermingled assertions with the factual statements that are speculative in nature and there are statements of innuendo sprinkled throughout.'' These statements could damage Dana and Joel's right to a fair trial, O'Neill said.

That was a somewhat odd position to take; after all, it had been O'Neill who had approved the warrants and the affidavits in the first place. Now the same judge who approved them seemed to be saying at least some of the information proffered to gain their approval was suspect. But the fact remained, continued O'Neill, not all the information contained in the affidavits was speculative; those parts of the affidavits that contained facts, not conjecture, was still sufficient to support the issuance of the warrants.

Based on O'Neill's ruling, the information used to justify the arrests would remained sealed for the foreseeable future.

Late in April, Dana's last hope to retain Berman for his defense attorney was dashed in an Ohio court. Dana's aunt, Betty Whitted, agreed not to provide any money from Austin Sr.'s estate to help Dana pay for his defense.

Dana Ewell, the boy who had everything, now had a public defender as his lawyer.

Peter Jones, one of the chief deputies of that embattled office, was assigned to represent Dana. In a way, Jones was a bit like John Souza: whatever would happen next, the

Ewell case would occupy most of his life for the next few years.

The major requirement, Jones soon learned, was to digest the enormous volume of information the Sheriff's Department had accumulated on the case over the previous three years. This would be no simple task, given the tens of thousands of pages of documents that had already been produced, and that the Sheriff's Department was still producing.

In fact, Jones had never seen a case like this before, with so much at stake—the very lives of two defendants, not to mentions millions of dollars, and a family turned against one of their own.

The first test, Jones knew, would come in the preliminary hearing—the proceeding where a judge must decide, after hearing the outlines of the evidence, whether enough evidence exists to warrant a full trial.

From where Jones was sitting, while it might look bad for Joel Radovcich, it was going to be an awful lot harder to prove that Dana Ewell had anything to do with the murders.

39

As the spring progressed, and the outlines of the case against Dana and Joel emerged, it became clear to the two defense lawyers, Terrence Woolf and now Peter Jones, that however much their clients had been friends in the past, a parting of interests was inevitable.

Indeed, from Dana's point of view, the sooner the parting, the better.

For one thing, while the District Attorney's office intended to use physical evidence to link Joel to the murders—the ballistic testing of Boudreau, Haag, and the FBI, along with the barrel of the gun unearthed with Jack's cooperation—the case against Dana was more tenuous.

Indeed, the strongest piece of evidence against Dana was amorphous—plain common sense. What other possible motive would Joel have had for killing Dana's family, besides the obvious—money from Dana Ewell? But common sense wasn't listed in the evidence code as a form of admissible evidence. Instead, the case against Dana was entirely circumstantial—the gathering of events that, taken together, clearly implied that Dana was part and parcel of a conspiracy.

The circumstantial evidence was powerful but not overwhelming. The telephone and financial records showed interaction between Dana and Joel, and the fact that those contacts continued even after the detectives told Dana they believed Joel was responsible for the killings was an important suspicious circumstance. The fact that Dana had given money to Joel and had apparently paid for his flying lessons was similarly suspicious. But when it came down to definitive evidence, the investigators had only one thing going for them: Jack Ponce.

And because Jack had never met Dana Ewell, his only knowledge of Dana's culpability came through Joel himself—what Joel told Jack about Dana. Because Jack's version of the story could be attacked in a variety of ways, basing the case against Dana on Jack's testimony was a bit like balancing a ten-story building on the tip of a single stick—and if the stick turned out to be straw, the whole thing would collapse.

In turn, that meant the defense strategies of Woolf and Jones would be radically different.

Where Woolf needed to attack the reliability of the ballistics evidence, Jones needed to attack the credibility of Jack Ponce, and the detectives' inferences from the surveillances that Dana was somehow involved.

Indeed, it was conceivable that Jones might advance the notion that even if the evidence showed Joel pulled the trigger, it was possible—even plausible—that Joel had done so without any involvement of Dana; that, in effect, the murders were the work of Joel and possibly Jack as part of a plot to isolate Dana, in order to somehow take advantage of him in the aftermath of the murders.

In other words, it might be possible to argue that Dana was Joel's dupe, rather than the other way around.

The conflict between defense strategies would eventually lead Dana's side to ask that his case be completely severed from Joel's.

If that happened, the District Attorney's office would face a number of evidentiary problems it would otherwise prefer not to have to confront.

But if the two defense lawyers might foresee the future need for their clients to confront one another, a more immediate problem developed: neither Woolf nor Jones wanted the preliminary hearing to take place, at least right then. They said they needed more time.

By the middle of August 1995, Joel and Dana had been in jail for more than six months. Slowly but surely, all of the voluminous records of the three-year investigation were making their way over to the defense lawyers.

There were, Woolf and Jones discovered, mammoth volumes of material—thousands of pages of reports, financial records, telephone records, statements of witnesses from five different counties, a number of states, fifty audio tapes, several video tapes, and more than twelve hundred still photographs. All of this stuff needed to be read, evaluated, and checked for accuracy before the defense could even hope to defend Dana and Joel.

Worse, Woolf and Jones discovered that several critical pieces of information still hadn't been turned over. One of the most crucial areas involved reports by the Arizona firearms expert, Lucien Haag. Although Haag had certified Boudreau's firearms analysis in December 1994, he was still doing tests.

The ballistics evidence, of course, was the critical evidence against Joel. How could he defend his client, Woolf asked, if he didn't know what the independent examiner had concluded about Boudreau's work? How could he hire his own expert to evaluate Haag's analysis?

Jones's problem was different. After all, the evidence against Dana was based on inferences by the detectives, buttressed by Jack's description of Joel's supposed confession at the beach. The detectives reasoned that Dana stood to gain a substantial sum of money from the murders, and that only Dana was in a position to provide the information necessary to Joel to commit the crimes; and further, the evidence of their association before and after the murders supported the likelihood of the detectives' inferences, which in turn were buttressed by Jack's assertions.

To undercut these inferences, Jones needed to show how detectives had jumped to improper conclusions; and further, that Jack had a motive to cast the blame away from himself and onto Dana.

And there was some indication of at least the first instance—conclusion-jumping and unfounded speculation, Jones argued. Hadn't the very same judge who approved the search warrants refused to unseal them, noting that the affidavits in support of the warrants contained unfounded speculation and conclusions?

Even the arrest warrants were flawed with "obvious distortions of the truth," Jones contended; the detectives were so anxious to hang the crime on Dana Ewell they had mangled the meaning of their own reports.

That was why, Jones said, he was demanding that the surveilling detectives produce any notes they had taken of the various telephone conversations that had supposedly been conducted between Joel and Dana.

Until they received these materials, Woolf and Jones said, they would not be prepared to proceed with the case. Late in August, at a hearing, both Woolf and Jones asked for a delay in the preliminary hearing until the additional materials could be provided.

"The arrest warrant affidavit that was submitted to get a judge's signature to arrest Mr. Ewell," Jones told Municipal Court Judge Victor Papadakis, "contains clear evidence of obvious distortions of the truth that can easily be shown.

"It won't even be difficult to show this at this time," Jones continued. "And that's why we're going to need those notes. That is why we're going to need all of the surveillance reports and that is why we're going to need all the known records.

"Let me give the court an example, and if need be, call Detective Souza. In [the] arrest warrant affidavit, for example, there's a representation that there's a telephonic conversation between codefendant Joel Radovcich and my client, Dana Ewell. That representation contains statements that Mr. Radovcich makes, allegedly [to] Mr. Ewell."

Jones was talking about the May 14, 1993, telephone

call, the one that appeared to mash together several conversations into one.

"And those statements are represented to be one phone call between Mr. Radovcich and Dana Ewell. The contents of that one-sided conversation . . . is construed to be incriminating. It's construed to be at least circumstantially incriminating. And there's just no question it's one of the reasons an arrest warrant [was issued]. . . ."

The problem, Jones said, was that while Detective Souza in the arrest warrant affidavit made it appear that all of the overheard remarks were part of a single conversation, the reports of the surveilling officers indicated that Joel had actually made several telephone calls.

"Now obviously," Jones went on, "they're [the surveillors] not going to hear everything, they're each going to take separate notes. If you compare what one officer heard from another, you can still—they're talking about the same thing, but the words change. But even then, the most important and significant thing is that these conversations . . . something about 'I miss you, I love you,' and implying that my client had this kind of relationship with Mr. Radovcich absolutely could not have been a conversation with Dana Ewell. And yet that's how it's represented in the arrest warrant affidavit."

That's why he wanted the officers' notes, Jones said— to demonstrate that the detectives had sifted through a variety of phrases by Joel Radovcich, some of them not even uttered to Dana Ewell, in an effort to construct a highly selective pastiche of seemingly incriminating statements in order to incriminate Dana.

"Now, we want the officers' notes," Jones went on. "We need them on all five other telephone conversations . . . we don't have surveillance reports—any reports on one of those conversations."

Nor, said Jones, had the defense received the telephone records accompanying the surveilled conversations.

"I need those phone records," Jones said. "I believe they could be exculpatory. I believe they could be exculpatory as I just think [we] demonstrated with at least one phone call, where we have multiple surveillance reports, that there are serious problems with the arrest warrant affidavit.''

The whole problem, Jones said, was that there was so much paper involved in the case that every time the defense was given something new, new questions arose as to whether there was still more to be had.

"In other words," Jones said, "we don't even know what we don't know. We get a report and it triggers something that, gee, there must be another report out there we don't have yet. I mean, that's how vast the discovery's been on this case.''

And Woolf wanted Haag's reports. Otherwise, he said, he wouldn't be prepared for the preliminary hearing.

"There are going to be two key elements to the prosecution's preliminary hearing presentation," Woolf told Judge Papadakis. "[The] first one is going to have to do with the ballistics evidence, and the second part is going to have to do with the only witness (the prosecution) is certain . . . to call . . . which would be Mr. Ponce.

"Mr. Ponce is being kept in D.A. custody, in effect, apparently the Holiday Inn or something like that, and to make sure he's around for the preliminary hearing, at which time he'll presumably be released because they anticipate they'll always have his preliminary hearing testimony to use at the time of trial.

"Now, because of that situation, this preliminary hearing may, in fact, be the trial in a large degree with respect particularly to this key witness. And under those kind of circumstances, I think it's essential as a matter of due process that we have full discovery before the preliminary hearing. This is not the normal situation. This is a highly unusual case and it's being handled in a highly unusual manner by the government. The ballistics testing, I'm informed, is not even going to be completed by mid-September.''

Then Woolf dropped his bomb. If he didn't get the Haag

ballistics reports before the preliminary hearing, Woolf said, he wouldn't be able to properly cross-examine Jack Ponce. If he wasn't able to cross-examine Jack, Woolf continued, Joel's right to confront witnesses against him would be unfairly limited. And that, Woolf did not need to add, could be grounds for reversal if Joel was ever convicted.

Judge Papadakis listened to the defense arguments, and then made his decision: the preliminary hearing would be continued for just two weeks. If Woolf didn't feel ready to cross-examine Jack by that time, well, that was his decision.

40

In 1990, the voters in California, in an effort to speed up the justice system, went to the polls and approved a sweeping revision of some of the most basic aspects of the state's penal code.

Known as Proposition 115, the changes for the first time required evenhandedness in discovery—that is, the process of letting the other side know what was to be submitted as evidence. But perhaps more importantly, although less noticed, Proposition 115 radically changed the way preliminary hearings were to be conducted. After passage of Proposition 115, prosecutors were permitted to make far more extensive use of hearsay in preliminary hearings than they had before.

Outside of the ballistics information and the financial and telephone records, the entire case against Joel and Dana was comprised of hearsay evidence—and not just ordinary hearsay, but often double and triple hearsay—what one person heard that another person said to a third person, for example.

There were, for example, the supposed statements made by Joel over the telephone—those overheard by the surveilling detectives.

And there were the statements supposedly made by Joel to Jack, both before and after the murders, that Jack had recounted to the detectives.

And, finally, there were the statements supposedly made by Dana to Joel, who allegedly repeated them to Jack, who in turn told them to the detectives.

All of this was hearsay evidence.

The whole subject of hearsay evidence starts out simply enough. According to the California Evidence Code, " 'Hearsay evidence' is evidence of a statement that was made other than by a witness while testifying at the hearing and that is offered to prove the truth of the matter stated."

In other words, statements made by witnesses outside of the courtroom are defined as hearsay if they are intended to prove the truth of what someone supposedly said—like the statements Joel was said to have made while conducting a conversation at a pay telephone.

And the law is quite specific about hearsay: "Except as provided by law, hearsay evidence is inadmissible."

It is a virtual certainty that any time a statute begins with the words, "except as provided by law," matters are going to become complex very quickly, and such is the case with hearsay. Indeed, within one page of the evidence code, exceptions to the hearsay rule begin to appear, and they are as many as they are arcane.

Hearsay evidence can be allowed to attack the credibility of a witness; it can be allowed if it was made as part of a confession or admission, or in furtherance of a conspiracy; if it was against the interest of the person who made the statement; if it is inconsistent with testimony given during a hearing; if it is a statement made to explain an act or event, or is a dying declaration; or if it is a statement of a mental state, including motive or intent; if it is about a will, or a business or official record; or if it concerns reputation in the community. As can be seen, there are far more exceptions to the rule against hearsay than there are prohibitions.

There is also an exception to the exceptions:

"A statement that is otherwise admissible [because of one of the above exceptions] as hearsay evidence is inadmissible against the defendant in a criminal action if the statement was made, either by the defendant, or by another, under such circumstances that it is inadmissible against the defendant under the Constitution of the United States or the State of California.''

Because Jack's version of the events of the murders had his knowledge coming from Joel Radovcich, that meant Dana had the constitutional right to confront his codefendant, Joel, about the veracity of this supposed statement. It was a right under the U.S. Constitution, as well as the state constitution. But Joel also had rights: he had, among others, the Fifth Amendment right to not be compelled to testify.

Did this mean that Joel's supposed statement to Jack— that he and Dana were going to split the inheritance—was admissible against Joel, but not Dana?

Absolutely, said Jones, Dana's lawyer. Any statement supposedly made by Joel recounting alleged statements made by Dana could not be allowed against Dana Ewell— unless Joel himself was willing to take the stand.

Asked if he was willing to allow Joel to testify, Woolf was quick:

"Not on your life," he said.

This was tricky, indeed. Oppliger, the senior deputy district attorney presenting the case, was forced to concede that the statements Jack had attributed to Dana through Joel could not be used against Dana under ordinary circumstances.

But, said Oppliger, they were still admissible against Joel himself; and once he'd proven that it was likely Joel had committed the crime, it would also be possible to argue that the only reason Joel had committed the crime was because of Dana's instigation, and that, therefore, the statements would be admissible because they were in furtherance of a conspiracy between Joel and Dana.

Why else would Joel have murdered three people he didn't know and would otherwise have cared less about?

Not so fast, said Jones. This was bootstrapping: proving A existed because of B, and proving B existed because of A. In effect Oppliger was claiming Dana had to be involved in the murders because Dana knew Joel, and that Joel had to be involved in the murders because he knew Dana. Oppliger, Jones said, was trying to prove the conspiracy by using the statements, and using the conspiracy to permit the statements to be used. There had to be independent evidence of a conspiracy, Jones said, and that didn't exist.

Finally, still another exception to the hearsay rule was passed into law by Proposition 115. With the passage of the measure, it now became permissible for police officers with more than five years' experience to provide hearsay testimony in a preliminary hearing.

This meant Souza could take the stand and testify to what he had been told by other people—whether he personally knew if what the other people told him was true or not. Thus, because of this exception to the hearsay rule, the defense would be unable to cross-examine the actual surveilling officers to determine the truth of the hearsay they said they had overheard. They'd have to take Souza's word for it.

The net effect of these hearsay exceptions was to give a substantial advantage to the prosecution, and to make it almost impossible for the defense to claim that there was no probable cause to believe Joel and Dana had committed the crimes.

On September 6, 1995, Judge Papadakis opened the preliminary hearing, and if the objective of the hearing was simple—to demonstrate whether crimes had been committed, and whether there was reason to believe that Dana and Joel had committed them—the legal maneuverings by the defense were not.

For one thing, Woolf's earlier objection to proceeding had created a tricky constitutional problem. In addition to the confrontation problem, if Woolf refused to cross-examine Jack, the groundwork might be laid for an appeal by Joel based on ineffective assistance of counsel.

Indeed, there were some who believed that Woolf had seized on this very prospect as a strategy to defend Joel—

sort of like calling an artillery strike down upon his own position.

"Mr. Woolf," Judge Papadakis asked, "are you prepared to proceed?"

"No, your honor," Woolf said, "I am not."

Without access to Haag's reports, Woolf said once again, it would be impossible to adequately defend his client. He made a new attempt to have the hearing postponed; the judge rejected it.

Oppliger began by proving that crimes had been committed, an essential element to move the case on to Superior Court for trial. He called Detective Melinda Ybarra, who described the scene in the Ewell house on the day the murders were discovered.

Oppliger asked Ybarra whether she was able to find any evidence of forced entry.

"I was not able to locate any such point," Ybarra said.

"How do you define forced entry?"

"There are many ways," Ybarra said. "You can have pry tool marks. You can break a window. You can kick a door down. Things of that nature." None of those things were present at the Ewell house, Ybarra noted.

Ybarra told how Dana Ewell had been observed removing the key from the awning of the backyard shed several days after the murders. The action, she said, seemed to be surreptitious. The inference was obvious: Dana had planted a key to the house in the shed for Joel to find and use.

Next, Oppliger had Ybarra describe the location and condition of the bodies. It was obvious that Dale Ewell had just entered the house before he was shot.

"Beneath the body," Ybarra said, "and at the decedent's feet, Dale Ewell, there were newspapers, a magazine, mail, a fax, broken pair of sunglasses. On Mr. Ewell's back there appeared to be little white specks of plaster, similar to the acoustical material you see on ceilings in homes. That was on his back, in back of his shirt, back of his head and around the carpet around his head. And there was a broken eyeglass around his head on the carpet."

Ybarra had accompanied the bodies to the medical examiner's office, and had attended the autopsies. Dale Ewell, she said, had been shot in the back of the neck. The bullet had exited from Dale's face just below his right eye.

Glee had been shot four times, Ybarra said, three times to the arm and torso, and once in the head.

"She too was fully clothed," Ybarra said, "she was wearing her eyeglasses, and she had a set of keys clutched in her right hand."

Ybarra was asked to describe Tiffany's body.

"She's lying facedown in the kitchen near a kitchen table and again, her arms are underneath—both her hands are underneath her torso, her elbows are bent and her hands are underneath her torso."

"Does that have any significance to you, the particular location you've described these two victims [Dale and Tiffany] with the hands?" Oppliger asked.

"Yes," Ybarra said.

"What, if any, significance does that have, to you?"

"Walking, caught unaware, shot, and went straight down."

There wasn't much either Woolf or Jones could do with Ybarra, but they tried.

Woolf questioned Ybarra about the alarm that hadn't gone off. There was no evidence to suggest that it had been turned on when the Ewells left for the beach, was there?

No, Ybarra said, acknowledging the implication that the killer did not necessarily have to know the alarm code to get inside the house.

Jones got Ybarra to admit that she hadn't noted the box of 9-millimeter ammunition in the bedroom in an early version of her report; still, there was no disputing the fact that photographs taken of the bedroom after the murders were discovered showed the box of 9-millimeter ammunition was present.

Jones wasn't denying that the ammunition was there; instead, he was playing a longer game. He was hoping to show, eventually, that the police search of the house—the one that resulted in the photograph—may have been an improper search, without a warrant, or without Dana's consent. That way, he reasoned, he might be able to get the box of ammunition thrown out as evidence if and when the case came to trial.

"Whenever you go to a scene," Jones asked, "it is important to make sure you catch every little detail, isn't it?" Jones asked.

"As much as humanly possible, yes," Ybarra said.

"You never know when one little detail might—might lead to uncovering something very significant about a case, isn't that right?"

"That's true."

"Were you there when there was a dusting for fingerprints?"

"Yes."

"To your knowledge, do you know if an alarm pad was ever dusted for fingerprints?"

"I can't remember at this time."

"Now when you walked through and you went into Dana Ewell's bedroom, you noticed a—a clock that was blinking on and off?"

"Yes, sir. On the nightstand."

"Your report indicates it appeared the power had been turned off; is that correct?"

"Uhm—just from personal knowledge I know that that occurs, power goes off, it comes back on, your alarm clocks will flash on 12:00."

"And that is what you observed to be happening in Dana's room?"

"Yeah. Flashing on the 12:00."

The implication was clear: at some point between the Ewells' departure and the discovery of their bodies five days later, the power to the Ewell house might have been turned off. If the power had been turned off, the burglar alarm might not work.

Next, Jones induced Ybarra to admit that she personally

hadn't checked the bathroom skylights. She'd only been told they were sealed shut, hadn't she? Jones asked. Yes, Ybarra said. And she hadn't actually checked herself, by standing on the bathroom sink, had she?

No, Ybarra said. And if someone turned off the power to the house, had come in through the skylight in the bathroom, he could then get to the master alarm pad to disable it, and thus all the motion detectors in the house, Jones implied by his questioning.

So this was another theory of the crime—one that did not require Dana's participation, if indeed the killer could turn off the alarm and get into the house by himself. If that was the case, Dana Ewell might well be innocent.

After Ybarra, Oppliger called John Souza.

41

This was Souza's moment, his vindication. After more than three years, after thousands of miles on the road, after interminable telephone calls; after the sneers and the insults from Dana and Joel, with the constant intimation that he was too stupid—this was Souza's hour of triumph. Souza came onto the witness stand determined to explain.

Suddenly finding oneself the center of attention, as Souza did on taking the witness stand, can be unnerving. In his testimony, Souza seemed eager to give his information—perhaps too eager. Later, some officials connected with the investigation conceded that Souza, despite his vast knowledge of the case, did not make a good witness.

But because Souza was one of the two lead investigators on the case, his testimony was needed by Oppliger to tie together a wide variety of circumstantial evidence.

Oppliger began by eliciting Souza's opinion that the burglary had been staged.

"My final conclusion was it was a staged burglary," Souza said.

"And what did you base that conclusion on, Detective Souza?"

"A number of things, lack of forced entry, the type of items that were placed on the sheet, the use of sheets in lieu of pillow cases, the total ransacking. Probably, I will consider, the most ransacked residence I've ever been into, burglary-wise, by far, way over—an overkill on the searching of the residence.''

The fact that the drawers had been searched by the burglar from the top down was particularly significant, Souza said.

''What do you mean by 'bottom up' to 'top down'?''

''Well,'' said Souza, ''If you search from the top down you have—when you open a drawer up to search that drawer, in order to get to the second drawer below it you would have to initially close or partially close the top drawer to see what's in the second drawer, without removing the drawers completely. By searching from the bottom up, you open your drawer, you search, you open the next drawer above it and search, and nothing's blocking your view of the search. Is that clear enough?''

Yes, said Oppliger. He then turned to the background investigations of Dana and Joel.

Joel Radovcich's name first surfaced in the investigation, Souza said, when he was interviewing a Santa Clara University dormitory resident assistant.

''In response to a question of who was Dana Ewell's friends, she responded that he didn't have too many friends and that there was one particular individual, that they were extremely close or appeared to be extremely close friends,'' Souza said.

''Who was that person—or, who did she tell you was that person?''

''Joel Radovcich.''

''And what, if anything, did she specifically indicate led her to that conclusion?''

''That she'd seen them on campus in and about the dorm area. They lived in the same dorm together. And that she felt it was an extremely odd relationship due to the fact that Dana was a very prim and proper type of student and where Joel was considered [the kind] that would go around on a skateboard and wear cut-off Levis and was considered basically—or to her, was like a goober.''

''Could you spell that?'' Woolf interjected.

*   *   *

Souza went on to discuss the interviews he and Ernie Burk
held with Dana during the first few days of the investigation. Dana told them he'd prepared a financial analysis of
the Ewell family's assets in January 1992, and that he'd
done this for his father. The analysis showed a net worth
of more than seven million dollars, Souza said.

Dana also told him, Souza said, that the last time he'd
seen the missing Browning pistol had been around Christ-
mas of the year before, when Dana and Dale had gone
shooting with the pistol.

Now Oppliger turned to Dana's possible motive.

"Did you talk with anyone that indicated . . . whether or
not Dana Ewell had—how would I put this—a love of
money or an obsession with money?"

"Yes," Souza said. "Sean Shelby, for one." Shelby had
told him Dana was obsessed with wanting to make a large
sum of money, Souza said. Nor was Shelby the only person
to make that observation about Dana, Souza said. So had
Joanne Slinkard, a longtime friend of Glee Ewell.

"She was personal friends with Glee Ewell," Souza said,
"to the length of, prior to even Dale and her, Glee Ewell,
getting married . . . that she watched Dana being raised and
that her perception of Dana was the fact that he received
everything from his parents, but it was never enough."

Next Souza was asked about the wills of Dale and Glee.
Oppliger wanted to establish the fact that Dana wouldn't
be able to get all the money from the estate right away. But
Jones, Dana's lawyer, threw up a storm of objections to
these questions on hearsay grounds, which were overruled.

After a break for lunch, Oppliger pulled a surprise: he
wanted to call his next witness out of order—Peter Radovcich. Souza would be recalled later, Oppliger said.

He was, Peter acknowledged, Joel's brother.

"During this period of time [from December 1991 to
Joel's arrest in 1995] did you ever know your brother to
have a job?" Oppliger asked.

"No," said Peter.

"Did you know, based on your contacts with your brother between his graduation and the time of his arrest, whether he had any other source of income other than a job?"

"Odds and ends. Working at my mom's house."

"Were you aware from your contacts with your brother, Joel, as to whether he had any outside source of income, such as investments, bonds, et cetera?"

"No."

"Your answer would be, no, he did not have—to your knowledge—have other sources of income?"

"Correct. Yeah, he did not," Peter said.

"Did Joel ever borrow money from you?"

"No."

"Do you know, sir, how Joel provided for his living expenses?"

"No."

"Did you sometimes see Joel with cash in hand, so to speak?"

"Sometimes."

"And did you see him, for instance, with hundred-dollar bills, and other denominations?"

"It would be an accumulation of twenties, maybe a hundred here, that's about it," Peter said.

But, Oppliger persisted, did Peter ever see Joel with a large sum of cash—"show-off money," Oppliger called it.

"No," said Peter.

Oppliger paused frequently to look over his notes. Peter was a tricky witness because he was Joel's brother, and thus potentially hostile. On the other hand, Peter had avoided being charged with his own involvement in the murders by agreeing to testify truthfully. Oppliger had to make sure that he framed his questions carefully in order to avoid giving Peter the opportunity to hedge his responses by taking a question literally. That way, Peter might still tell the truth, but add nothing. Oppliger intended to ease into the area of the silencers, and he didn't want any slip-ups.

"Prior to 1992," Oppliger asked, "had you ever assisted your brother in the modification of a weapon?"

"Yes."

In response to Oppliger's probing, Peter described welding the pipe extension onto the .380 Llama pistol—Joel's first silencer experiment.

"What was this modification you assisted on? What was the purpose of this modification?"

"To create a silencer," Peter said.

"Why did you weld that piece on?"

"Because I was asked to."

"And who asked you to weld that piece on?"

"My brother."

"And when he asked you to do that, did you say anything to him, like 'Why?' "

"No."

Now Oppliger moved to the day of the murders. Had Joel ever told him he was at the auto body shop on the day of the murders?

No, said Peter.

Well, said Oppliger, he'd discussed the investigation with others, hadn't he?

"Yes. My mom, family, and my brother."

"How about Mr. Ponce?"

"Yes."

"Would it be fair to say you were aware this was a murder investigation?"

"Yes."

"And did you have occasion to ask your brother, 'Where were you on April 19 of 1992?' "

"No."

"Is there some reason that you—since he was a suspect, that you didn't have occasion to say, 'Joel, where were you on April 19th of 1992?' "

"No," said Peter, "because I knew where he was."

Whoops. This wasn't in the game plan. Suddenly Peter

seemed to be suggesting he might be able to provide an alibi for Joel on the day of the murders.

"Now, you knew where he was," Oppliger said. "Let's go to that. On April 19, 1992—let's move to the eighteenth. Okay?"

"Okay."

"On the eighteenth you and your wife did something?"

"Yes."

"What was that?"

"We went to Knott's Berry Farm for her birthday."

"And did you spend the night down there?"

"Yes, we did."

"And then on Sunday, the nineteenth, did you return to your residence?"

"Yes."

"Can you give me your best estimate as to when you arrived home?"

"Between nine and eleven in the morning."

"And at that point in time, was Joel there?"

"Yes."

Joel had been watching Peter and Danielle's dog overnight, Peter said. He left after they arrived.

Of course, if this were true, that meant if Joel was the killer, he would have had to drive to Fresno and enter the Ewell house in broad daylight, only a few hours before the Ewells were due to return home. That certainly wasn't Jack's version of the story, at least as he claimed that Joel had told him.

What time did Joel return to Peter's apartment? Oppliger asked.

"Between nine and eleven at night," Peter said.

"Did you see Joel at any time between?"

"In between? No."

Now Oppliger veered back to the gun modifications performed by Peter.

"Did you have occasion to perform some work on the barrel of a second gun?"

"Yes."

"And what, if anything, did you do?"

"I welded a washer onto the barrel." The washer, Peter said, was placed about six to eight inches down from the tip of the barrel. Joel had asked him to do it, Peter said.

"Did you say, 'Joel, why do you want me to weld a washer onto this gun barrel?' "

"No."

"Why not?"

"I didn't have a concern to do it."

"Did you have a thought in mind as to—in your own mind as to what the purpose of your act was—or what you were seeking to accomplish by modifying the barrel?"

"I had my own thought, yes."

"What did you have in your own mind?"

"That it was for a silencer."

"And along that line, in your own mind, were you aware that a silencer for a weapon is illegal?"

"At that time, no."

After more questions and answers, in which Oppliger forced Peter to admit that he'd heard Joel testing the silenced weapon, and still had not asked his brother what he was up to, Oppliger asked Peter if, before April of 1992, he had ever heard of a gun called a Featherlight AT9.

"No," Peter said.

"At some point in time did you become familiar with the name of such a weapon?"

"Yes."

"And when was that?"

"I don't know the time, but it's—Detective Souza brought it to my attention."

In fact, Peter said, he'd never seen the assembled gun, either before April 19, 1992, or after. It wasn't until Souza showed him a photograph of the gun and told him it was an AT9 that Peter knew what one was supposed to look like.

After another series of questions relating to Joel's alleged testing of the silenced weapon elicited little new information, Oppliger turned to the evening of April 22, 1992—the day Joel said he'd received the get-out-of-town code.

"Did you have occasion," Oppliger asked Peter, "to where Joel came to you in a panic state? Or schizoid, or however you want to indicate, worried?"

"I'm not sure of the time, but he did come to me."

"What, if anything, did Joel say to you?"

"He wanted me to take him someplace."

"Can you give me your best recollection as to what it was that he said?"

"That he'd gotten a code and that he needed to go."

"Did you ask him, 'Joel, why don't you just get in your car and go?' "

"Yeah."

"And what, if anything, did he say to you?"

"Nothing. He left after I told him I couldn't take him anywhere."

"You said you couldn't or wouldn't?"

"Could not. Would not."

"And why not?"

"Because I was a bit scared at the time and I had my wife upstairs."

"But—you know what I'm going to ask next, don't you? What were you scared of?"

"He was unnerved. He's usually a pretty calm person."

"It was his appearance that scared you?"

"His attitude."

"And can you be a little bit more specific, if you're able to, about his attitude that led you to a state of fear?"

"He was scared."

"Did you ask him what he was scared of?"

"No."

"Maybe this seems overly confrontive," Oppliger said, "but it seems like, he's your brother, you love him, and he was afraid. And my question would be, why didn't you ask?"

"I didn't want to know," Peter said.

42

When testimony resumed, Oppliger led Peter through the subsequent events of the evening—when he and Jack had driven through the San Fernando Valley, throwing away things from the backpack Joel had given him a few days before.

Peter described how he and Jack had driven from Dumpsters to storm drains, and then into various canyons, pitching out parts of guns, a pair of tennis shoes, books about guns, and some pieces of tennis balls, while his wife Danielle repeatedly paged him. At the end, the only thing left was the gun barrel.

"After you returned to your place," Oppliger asked, "may I assume that based on what you have previously stated, your wife was immediately angry with you?"

"Yes."

"And did Jack leave—"

"Yes."

"—right away? Did you see him leave?"

"I didn't see him drive off. I saw him walk out the door and that was it."

The next day, after Oppliger had Peter clarify some of the remarks he'd made to the detectives after his arrest on March 8, 1995, it was time for Peter's cross-examination.

And this is where the constitutional problems forecast earlier by Woolf first blew up.

"Your honor," Woolf said, "the court has previously denied my motion for a continuance so that I can have ballistic test results from law enforcement investigation and consult with my own ballistics experts on the matter.

"This witness's testimony having been primarily concerned with firearms evidence, I can't intelligently cross-examine him at this time, and I do not want a later court, on the basis of an incomplete examination, telling me I have exercised my right to cross-examine the witness. I have no questions."

Well, of course, many areas of Peter's testimony had nothing to do with ballistics, but rather Peter's observations about the actions and behavior of Joel, and equally important, Jack. But in opting not to cross-examine Peter, Woolf was playing his dangerous hole card, the artillery strike on his own position. In effect, he had chosen to destroy his defense in order to save it.

Oppliger leaped to his feet.

"Excuse me," he said, "I'm going to request that the court admonish Mr. Radovcich that—"

"The witness?" asked Judge Papadakis, confused.

"No, the defendant," Oppliger said. "That at this time he and his lawyer have the opportunity to cross-examine this witness, and if this witness were to die or [in] some other way become incapacitated and they fail to exercise their opportunity to cross-examine this witness, a court at a later date may, in fact, find that the opportunity to cross-examine was sufficient to meet the dictates of the confrontation clause of the United States Constitution. And that, therefore, he would be giving up, in essence, his right to cross-examination of this witness through a tactical maneuver, which may or may not be effective."

In other words, Oppliger wasn't going to idly allow Woolf to gum up the prosecution with an appealable issue. He wanted the judge to warn Woolf that any choice not to cross-examine Peter was completely voluntary—and a mere tactic at that.

Woolf wasn't having it.

"I think it's inappropriate for counsel to request the court to admonish my client with respect to anything," he said. "I have made this decision in consultation with Mr. Radovcich, and I have no problem putting on the record the fact that we have consulted with regard to the matter and have decided this was the only intelligent decision that is open to us."

The judge agreed with Woolf that it would be inappropriate to admonish—or warn—Joel that he could not later claim he was denied the right to cross-examine his brother; but Papadakis ordered Woolf to consult with Joel one more time to make sure that if they still refused to cross-examine Peter, "it will be a matter of strategy and good lawyering. . . ."

Following this exchange, Oppliger still wasn't ready to return to Souza. Instead, he called another witness out of order: Jack Ponce.

43

Was there anyone in the city of Fresno who didn't understand that Jack Ponce was the key witness against Dana Ewell—someone who Jack Ponce had never once met?

But it was true: Jack Ponce, 27 years old, career college student turned bartender, son of the prosperous retired dentist Dr. Ernest Ponce, alumnus of Chaminade High School and the University of California at Los Angeles, friend of Peter Radovcich, buyer of the gun used to assassinate Dale, Glee, and Tiffany Ewell, was at the very epicenter of his life.

For much of the spring Jack had been interviewed over and over again by various detectives, and by agents of the FBI; Jack tried to respond to the questions, but the detectives believed Jack wasn't trying hard enough. Indeed, as the spring turned into the summer, some began to wonder whether Jack hadn't been far more deeply involved than he was willing to admit.

Was it possible that Jack himself had been present in the Ewell house when the murders were committed? It didn't seem very likely. Certainly all of the victims had been shot with the same gun, which argued a single shooter. But Jack's vagueness, particularly when it came to questions involving Peter, continued to be a worry.

Then, in August, Jack was interviewed once more—this

time by Ed Hunt, the District Attorney himself.

An Air Force veteran and a career prosecutor, Hunt had a salty way of talking, and a tough demeanor. He carried a .45-caliber semiautomatic pistol on his belt, and he knew how to use it. He wasn't shy about telling people he wanted to see Joel and Dana get what they deserved: the death penalty. So Hunt wasn't about to let Jack turn into a noodle on the witness stand.

After talking with Jack for awhile, Hunt suddenly lost his temper with Jack's vagueness. Hunt produced an envelope, and from the envelope drew a number of still pictures of the dead Dale, Glee, and Tiffany. He threw them down in front of Ponce.

"This isn't any goddamn motorcycle theft," Hunt told Ponce. "Take a look at what your friend Joel did. Take a good look."

Jack looked at the pictures. He turned pale.

"After that," Hunt recalled later, "his memory got an awful lot better."

Now Jack's memory was to be tested once again, this time not only by the prosecutors, but also by Dana's public defender, Pete Jones. Joel's lawyer, Woolf, again refused to cross-examine, citing the same reasons he had given for not questioning Peter Radovcich.

But Public Defender Jones, at least, intended to give Jack a thorough going-over.

Oppliger's plan for Jack's testimony was fairly straightforward. He wanted Jack to show how the conspiracy between Joel and Dana had developed, and how Joel had planned and then executed the murders, and then, how he'd later confessed to Jack. To give Jack's account veracity, Oppliger wanted to use Jack's account of his own criminal actions as evidence of his truthfulness.

Jack began at the beginning. In the summer of 1991, he said, Joel had asked him to get a gun—one that would not have Joel's name on it. He'd given Joel the Llama pistol, and then went with Joel to the gun show in Anaheim, where

Joel bought the pipe for the barrel extension to be used as the first silencer. And at the gun show, Jack said, he and Joel had seen an AT9 Featherlight.

"Did Joel attempt to purchase an AT9 on that date?" Oppliger asked.

"Yes, he did."

"And was he successful?"

"No, he was not."

"Why not?"

"The gentleman who he was trying to purchase it from wanted more identification than—or any identification, and Joel just wanted to give him cash for it."

Later, Jack said, Joel had obtained a .22 Beretta pistol from him, and made a silencer for that gun, as well as the earlier experiment with the Llama. Jack said he'd seen Joel test the new silencer, and it worked.

The next time he heard from Joel, Jack said, was in March, when Joel called him at his girlfriend's apartment. Joel wanted him to buy an AT9, in Jack's name, because Joel didn't want his own name associated with the purchase.

When Joel called, said Jack, he was out of money. His father had cut him off, and he was leaving the apartment of his girlfriend. He wanted to buy a van from Peter's plumbing shop to live in. Joel offered him money for buying the gun, Jack said, and this was a chance to get half of the money needed to buy the van. So he agreed to buy the gun.

On March 23, 1992, Jack said, he went to the gun store and purchased the AT9. He filled out all the papers, paid by check, and agreed to return on April 8 to pick it up.

On the eighth, Jack said, he'd picked up the gun, along with an extra clip and a box of ammunition, and drove it to Peter's apartment. There, he said, he'd given it to Joel; even he knew, Jack said, that Joel intended to make a silencer for the deadly assault weapon.

Over the next day, Oppliger led Joel through the rest of the story: how Joel had gone to work to make the silencer;

how Joel had called him, perhaps a week later, to invite him to see the results of his handiwork.

Joel took him into the Radovcich family garage, Joel said, and retrieved the gun from a backpack on top of some shelves. Jack locked the door while Joel screwed the weapon together, including the new silencer. Then Joel fired into a log to demonstrate his creation.

"What did this silencer actually look like?" Oppliger asked.

"It was black PVC pipe."

"About how long was it?"

"Around a foot or—" Jack held out his hands. "Over a foot long. It was the whole length of the barrel. I don't remember how long the barrel was exactly, in inches, but the silencer engulfed the whole thing."

After a few more questions relating to Joel's silencer books from Paladin Press, Oppliger asked Jack whether he had known what the gun was to be used for.

"I didn't ask him," Jack said, "what it was going to be used for. I asked him if he was going to make a lot of money on it and he said, 'Yeah.' "

Jack said he thought that meant Joel was going to sell the gun and silencer to someone else, not commit murder with it.

Next Jack went through the events of the midnight ride, when, with Peter, he had disposed of the materials in the backpack.

"And when you finished disposing of these goods," Oppliger asked, "where did you go?"

"Back to Pete's apartment," Jack said.

"At this point in time, where is the barrel?"

"The barrel is the last thing we had. It was still in our possession."

"So you arrived at the apartment and the barrel—you still have the barrel?"

"Yes."

"What happens then?"

"Pete—I mean, his wife has been calling numerous

times, especially after the earthquake, and so he walked upstairs, or he was going upstairs; and I told him I would just get rid of it, and I walked over a couple of fields, which is a couple of blocks, and buried it.''

After a recess, Jack returned to the stand, this time with Oppliger intending to move into the most sensitive area of all—what Jack claimed Joel had told him in regard to Dana.

"He said," Jack told Oppliger, "that it had to do with eight million dollars, and he and the other guy were going to split it in half. He was saying the reasons for it.''

"The reasons . . . ?'' Oppliger prompted.

"For the homicides," Jack said.

"Well," Oppliger said, "did he make any further statements with respect to this same subject matter you were discussing?''

"About the division of the money, right?''

"Right," Oppliger said.

"He said we were going to assume the throne.''

Here was a statement of clearly critical importance, and yet none of the lawyers involved in the case saw the need to interject objections to obtain further clarity.

Most importantly, given the alternative scenarios of the murders, who was the "we" who were going to assume the throne?

Was this Jack's paraphrase of Joel's paraphrase of Dana's statement to Joel, that Dana and Joel were "going to assume the throne''?

Or—was it Jack's statement of Joel's statement *to him*—that, in other words, Joel was saying to Jack that *Joel and Jack were going to assume the throne*?

In other words—*who* was going to assume the throne?

Regrettably, none of the legal counsel followed this issue up appropriately. Neither Jones nor Woolf objected on foundational grounds, and Oppliger quickly moved on to another area.

After a few more minutes, Oppliger came to Joel's supposed confession to Jack—the one at the beach at Malibu on the day of the Rodney King riots. And at this point Oppliger ran head-on into the morass that was the hearsay rule and its exceptions and exceptions to exceptions.

"At this time," Oppliger told the judge, "I will be offering the confession of Joel Radovcich against Dana Ewell as a statement against penal interest. As an offer of proof, it will be essentially that I, Joel Radovcich, committed the Ewell triple homicide for one-half the inheritance."

Now, Jones wanted to keep this supposed confession of Joel to Jack out of the evidence. It seemed to him that Joel's supposed statements to Jack—at least those that implicated Dana—should be inadmissible as evidence under the exception to the exception: the law that made hearsay inadmissible if the maker of the supposed statement, Joel, was not available to be cross-examined.

Joel, obviously, would claim his right not to testify under the Fifth Amendment; to allow this multiple hearsay, from Dana to Joel to Jack, would violate Dana's rights under the Sixth Amendment to confront witnesses against him, Jones argued.

But Judge Papadakis said he believed that the statements attributed to Joel by Jack were admissible as evidence because they were statements made in furtherance of a conspiracy—i.e., between Joel and Jack, and presumably, Joel and Dana. He overruled Jones's objection.

"Did Joel tell you why he committed this murder?" Oppliger asked.

"Yes."

"And what did he say?"

"To split the inheritance."

"Did he tell you how much he believed the inheritance to be?"

"Yes."

"And what, if anything, did he say?"

"Eight million dollars."

"Did he say who he was going to split the money with?"

"Yes, he did."

"And who did he say he was going to split the money with?"

"Dana Ewell."

44

On the following Monday, after a series of cleanup questions from Oppliger, in which Jack said Joel told him that Dana had been providing him money, and admitted that he himself had received about a thousand dollars from Joel—more evidence of the conspiracy of three—it was Jones's turn to question Jack.

Jones's task with Jack was to demonstrate that Jack had his own reasons for lying about Dana's supposed involvement with the murders. To that end, Jones planned an attack on Jack's credibility as a witness. Moreover, Jones wanted to suggest, through Jack's anticipated answers, that the detectives had provided Jack with the information they wanted him to say.

"Now," said Jones, "when you were arrested . . . what time of day were you arrested?"

"Nighttime," said Jack.

"And you were booked for three counts of murder, is that correct?"

"Yes, that's correct."

"And you had a pretty good idea of what these murders involved, is that correct?"

"Yes."

"You knew it carried the death penalty, didn't you?"

"Yes."

Jones abruptly moved away from Jack's possible motive

for lying about Dana's involvement in the murders—to avoid the death penalty—and went back to Jack's first four interviews with the detectives, in late 1993 and early 1994.

"You indicated to Detectives Curtice and Souza that you'd never socialized with Joel Radovcich except at Peter Radovcich's house, is that correct?"

"I indicated that, yes."

"And that was a lie?"

"Yes, it was."

In the first interview he'd had with the detectives, Jack hadn't told them he'd owned an AT9, had he? Jones asked.

"Actually, I indicated that I had owned a 9-millimeter rifle at that time," Jack said, "but we had a miscommunication about that and that's one of the problems that Detective Souza and I had."

"You still believe you indicated to Detective Souza that you owned a 9-millimeter on that date?"

"Yes."

"Did you say it was an AT9?"

"No, I said I owned a 9-millimeter rifle, but it was messed up."

"And you told Detective Souza that you'd never obtained a gun for Joel Radovcich, is that correct?"

"Yes, I did."

"That was a lie?"

"Yes, it was."

"Now," said Jones, "Detective Souza brought up this lock pick?"

"Yes."

"That you had allowed, as you say, Joel Radovcich to have it sent to your house?"

"Yes."

"And you indicated that it was a locking device, that you really weren't sure what it was?"

"Yes."

"That was a lie, was it not?"

Yes, said Jack, it was.

On it went, with Jones dragging out every other lie Jack

had told the police over the year before he was arrested—
about Joel staying at his apartment for the summer, about
the purchase of the gun, about the frequency of his contact
with Joel, the false police report on the theft of the AT9,
the lies he'd told the detectives about getting the gun for
his birthday, wanting to shoot opossums in his mother's
attic, all of it. Jones was trying to make the point that because Jack had repeatedly lied before, he could well be
doing the same thing now.

Jones turned to Jack's prior criminal history.

"The reality is that you and Joel engaged in a number
of thefts that summer, isn't that correct?"

"Yes."

Oppliger objected to the questions, saying it wasn't rel-
evant to the murders.

"Your honor," said Jones, "I wish to demonstrate to the
court the extensive knowledge this witness, in all likelihood, has in engaging in thefts with a codefendant in this
case to show that their relationship was a rather, in all likelihood, a very close one to the point they were crime partners in a number of exploits, in that it would tend to show
that they might have had other criminal ambitions that went
beyond theft offenses."

In other words, Jones was suggesting, the plot to murder
the Ewell family could have been hatched by the previous
partners-in-crime, Joel and Jack, by themselves.

Judge Papadakis allowed the questions.

Throughout the rest of the day, Jones's cross-examination of Jack continued, demonstrating through Jack's answers that he had known many of the preliminaries of the
plot—the experiments on silencers, the purchase of the
weapon, the arrangements of pager codes, even down to
Joel providing money to Jack on several occasions.

Several times, Jones returned to Jack's relationship with
Souza, trying to show that Jack's seeming intimate knowledge of the murders could have come from the detective,
rather than Joel himself.

"In March, early March, you were placed under arrest

for three counts of murder. You've testified to that, correct?''

"Yes."

"At that time you were aware you could get the gas chamber for those charges, correct?"

"Yes."

"Was that the first time you have ever been in custody, Mr. Ponce?"

"Yes."

"Did you sleep that night?"

"No."

"Think about what you'd gotten yourself into?"

"Yeah," said Jack, "I've been thinking about that for awhile."

"First time you ever had handcuffs placed on you, Mr. Ponce?"

"Yes."

"Were you put into a holding cell?"

"I was put into a jail cell."

"Did you want to get out of that jail cell?"

"I just—did I want to get out?"

"Yes."

"Yes."

"And after spending the night in jail, thinking about possibly never getting out, did you think about what life in prison might be like?"

"Yes."

"Did you think about the death penalty?"

"Yes, I did."

"Were you afraid? Of being possibly locked in prison for a long, long time, possibly even receiving the death penalty?"

"Yes."

"At some point in time you informed the sheriff's detectives that you wanted to make a deal, right?"

"Some time during the day, yes."

"You mentioned you had some discussion on the way from San Bernardino to Fresno."

"Yes."

"Do you recall—were you asked questions, or did you just spontaneously make statements?"

"The only thing I remember is Detective Souza saying—I'm trying to remember his exact words—'It will go easier on you if you cooperate.' "

"You told him at that point in time you did not want to cooperate."

"I said I'd like to get a lawyer."

"What did you talk about?"

"On the way up? I talked about my family."

Soon Jones turned to the subject of the key evidence in the case—the gun barrel.

"Now," said Jones, "after dumping most of the parts, you held on to the barrel, is that correct, of the AT9?"

"Well, we—we were driving all over, trying to find good places for everything and that just happened to be the last piece, so . . ."

"Okay."

"I don't know if that constitutes holding on to it," Jack said. "It was the last thing we got rid of."

"And you just held on to it?"

"No. Peter—when we got back to his house, I just grabbed it and went and buried it."

"Was there a conscious effort on your part to place that barrel in a spot where you could go back and find it?"

"At the time it was just something that I—we didn't want to put anywhere where it would be found. And since we're—I don't know, because we were both new at that, that was the most important thing and we were very selective about putting it in a Dumpster. And so I knew it was an important part. That's how I labeled that."

After more questions about the AT9, and Jack's observations of Joel's preparations for making the silencer, Jones turned to the supposed confession Joel had made to Jack at the beach.

"This plan to go to the beach, was that your suggestion? Joel Radovcich's suggestion?"

"I don't know," said Jack. "We were just driving. I don't know how we ended up there."

"Just the two of you?"

"Yes."

"During the day?"

"Yes."

"Did you pack a picnic lunch?" Jones's tone was growing more sarcastic.

"No."

"You just kind of went and kicked back on the beach?"

"Yes."

"Do you always go to the beach with mass murderers?"

"I only know one, but—no. You mean—"

"He already told you he was involved in a triple homicide, you said, correct?"

"Yes."

"You knew what those guns had been used for, didn't you know, when you buried them?"

"The one gun?"

"Yes, the one gun."

"Yes."

"And, here a week later, you've invited him to stay at your place or your girlfriend's place, going to the beach with him? Is that what you're saying?"

"What exactly am I saying? That—"

"You knew, or you claim, at least, that Joel Radovcich had confided in you that he was involved in a mass murder?"

"Triple homicide," Jack said.

"And you invited him to stay at your girlfriend's apartment with you. You go to the beach together. At some point in time you put him up or helped him to a motel?"

"Yes."

"My point," Jones said, "is that when you—at the time you went to the beach, you felt comfortable with Joel Radovcich, didn't you?"

"Comfortable enough to go to the beach. Are you asking me what I was thinking of him at that time?"

"I'm not asking you anything now, Mr. Ponce," Jones said, implying that Jack, even though he knew Joel's terrible secret, wasn't in fear of his own life—possibly because only he and Joel had been the whole conspiracy all along.

45

The following day, Oppliger finally re-called Detective Souza to the witness stand, intending to go over the evidence from the surveillances. Here the problem of hearsay arose once more—in part because Souza himself had not done the surveillance, but relied upon the briefings given later by the surveilling officers.

In some cases, the oral briefings were at variance with the written surveillance reports, and as Jones had previously suggested, the written reports sometimes were at variance with notes taken by the surveilling officers.

In any event, Souza quickly ran into more difficulties when he couldn't remember exactly what had happened in which surveillance.

Oppliger tried to begin with the second surveillance date, when Joel and Dana were surreptitiously observed going to the bank.

"And where—what types of business or where did the observations—where did the surveillance observe the gray Cadillac . . . to go, after it left the Park Circle address?"

"This is tough," said Souza. "They went to a bank. They drove to the La Grand area [north of Fresno], went out into the fields, almond orchard in the La Grand area, later determined to be the Ewell farm in Merced County."

Jones objected. Souza was vague as to who had made the observations, he said.

Oppliger agreed with Jones. "I certainly agree. The last statement was unclear . . . just strike it for now. Then we can start over."

"Do you have your reports with you?" Oppliger asked.

"Yes, sir."

"Do you recall speaking with Detective Haroldsen?"

"That date?"

"On this particular date, the twenty-sixth?"

"Okay," said Souza. "The problem I'm having is there's a lot of dates and there's a lot of contact with the same individuals."

"Perhaps," interjected Woolf, "we should take a recess at this time and let the detective look at the reports."

"I was just thinking exactly the same thing," Judge Papadakis said.

Oppliger suggested that the defense lawyers start their cross-examination of Souza on other matters; that way, the rest of the day wouldn't be wasted. Souza, Oppliger said, could study the reports that night and return the following day prepared to give appropriate answers.

"He's going to work late," Oppliger said. "He's just not going to get off at four-thirty tonight."

After a short recess, Oppliger agreed to withdraw Souza from the stand once more, and go ahead with two more out-of-order witnesses.

He called Allen Boudreau, who recounted the unusual markings he'd seen at the base of the bullets, and how he'd gone to the Winchester plant in East Alton to find out what had caused them.

After meeting with the Winchester people, Boudreau said, he'd concluded that the marks had been made by a worn coning punch.

"Having reached that particular conclusion," Oppliger asked, "did that put you any closer to the conclusion you were asked to make?"

"No," Boudreau said. "It really didn't matter to me what tool made it. What was significant was it was a very small number of bullets. Their best estimate was no more than seven thousand five hundred bullets manufactured in 1971.''

''And what significance did that have to you?''

''That's a very, very small number.''

''And for the benefit of us, how is that significant in answering the pertinent question?''

''Well,'' said Boudreau, ''the murders occurred some twenty-one years later. Seventy-five hundred bullets loaded into some amount of ammunition, which was sold in the United States, may have been sold in Canada, may have been shipped overseas via international marketing, those seventy-five hundred rounds were clearly spread around a large geographic area. Twenty-one years later, there would probably be very little of that ammunition left.

''My opinion is that it's nearly certain that the murder bullets came from that box of ammunition,'' Boudreau concluded.

After a night studying the surveillance reports with Detective Souza, Oppliger was ready to try again with his effort to establish the circumstantial evidence that Dana and Joel had been in repeated contact from the time of the murders forward.

But again, just as Souza began describing the overheard conversations of April 1, 1993, Jones and Woolf objected.

It was not only hearsay, said Jones, but double hearsay—first it was Joel being overheard by the surveilling officer, then it was Souza giving hearsay as to what the surveilling officer had told *him*. It was irrelevant and without any legal basis, both Jones and Woolf insisted.

Worse, said Jones, besides the fact that there was no showing the first telephone call had been made to Dana Ewell, the fact that the conversation had lasted, according to the telephone records, for more than thirty-one minutes should give anyone pause as to the reliability of the report of the overheard information.

''It's a thirty-two-minute phone call,'' Jones said, ''[and] maybe bits and pieces, approximating forty-five seconds' worth, have been picked up, perhaps, by Sergeant Hollis. He doesn't know what order they were in . . . he would say he doesn't know what order they were in, how much time occurred between statements. The circumstances under which they are heard are so ambiguous, so subject to speculation, that they become irrelevant.''

No, Judge Papadakis said, he didn't think so. "I think I will allow it anyway,'' he said.

Oppliger plowed ahead, each time encountering a flurry of new objections from Woolf and Jones. Finally it appeared that Souza was growing confused as to how to best answer.

"I'm not sure I understand your question, sir,'' Souza told Oppliger at one point.

"Sir, do you have a report available to refresh your recollection?'' Oppliger asked. He was growing frustrated himself.

Thus, report by report, line by line, Oppliger tried to lead Souza through the minefield of potential objections thrown up by Woolf and Jones.

Finally, Jones asked that the evidence of the overheard conversations be thrown out because of foundational grounds—in other words, that because no one had proven who the calls were made to, there was no legal basis for accepting the evidence.

"A number of calls,'' Jones said, "that they have attributed to my client in ongoing reports, because of some location of pay phones . . . we have gotten phone records on them and can prove they were definitely not phone calls to my client at the times in question.''

At least some of the overheard conversations attributed to Dana Ewell, Jones insisted, "clearly and absolutely and definitely were not conversations with my client.''

But Oppliger said Jones and Woolf were wrong, that a foundation for the evidence did exist—the clone pager. The very fact that Joel's pager was given a number for Joel to call, and that Dana and Monica Zent had been seen in the vicinity of the pay telephone on the night that the detectives told Dana that they believed Joel was responsible for the murders showed that the two were in contact, and engaged in a conspiracy to cover up the murders.

Most important, regardless of the content of the conversations, the conversations showed post-murder contact between Joel and Dana, and that itself was enough to provide a legal foundation to believe a conspiracy existed.

Judge Papadakis agreed. The overheard conversations would be allowed in.

46

"What's the theory here?" Jones was arguing, on the last day of the hearing, that the charges against Dana Ewell should be dismissed.

"The theory here is that Mr. Ponce, a sick, false snitch, comes to court and says Joel Radovcich, who Detective Souza even says he didn't believe what Joel Radovcich told Mr. Ponce, in part, that what they want us to accept as perverted type of hearsay evidence to accuse Mr. Ewell of these murders.

"But the theory is that Mr. Ponce, for some reason, whatever Joel told him, was in furtherance of a conspiracy. . . .

"So first you have to believe Ponce, which is a stretch, and then you have to say, well, yeah, but . . . Joel Radovcich is an individual we can't even confront. You have to argue that what he said is truthful, and Mr. Souza said he didn't believe some of the things Ponce says Joel Radovcich said is true. . . .

"It's marginal circumstantial evidence. You have to view it with a jaundiced eye to derive incriminating evidence that tends toward Dana Ewell. They suggest some kind of kinky conspiracy. Detective Souza misquoted someone at Santa Clara University about this relationship, suggesting, I think some kind of kinky conspiracy instead of an ongoing friendship, which I surely think it was, that they want us to conclude that money spent on or at least lent to friends implies a conspiracy; that Dana's understandable reaction to being accused, to being followed, to being harassed by law enforcement suggests guilt instead of righteous indignation.

"And I think we showed all the ways his behavior would indicate lack of consciousness of guilt, that an inability to explain whether an alarm was on or off or had been circumvented and the possible use of bullets found at the scene proves some kind of sloppy inside job instead of a clever outside job.

"They want to assume that engaging in activities with friends, involving things he's done with his family his whole life, proves some kind of motive, instead of a young man trying to deal with a tragic loss, that small bits of one-sided conversations of the codefendant with someone in Santa Clara taken out of order, out of context by those who set out to get Dana Ewell, [to] prove guilt, instead of innocent conversation, possibly concerning police harassment. . . .

"We have here, your honor, a case with three and a half years, over a million dollars' worth of surveillance, expert consultation throughout the United States, and an investigation from a war chest the defense will never even see anything close to the likes of, we have the hearsay testimony of a sick false snitch representing multiple hearsay of somebody whose account Detective Souza doesn't even believe. In other words, we have what's left after all of this, a handful of weak inferences.

"I'm asking the court not to hold Dana Ewell to answer for the charges."

"Mr. Oppliger?"

"I think we have to begin, obviously, with the nature of the crime itself, and look to, what does this show us?" said Oppliger in his argument.

"And in this particular instance we have the Ewell family killed execution-style, leaving one heir to a seven-to-eight-million-dollar estate. It's clear from the physical evidence at the scene that the plan was to kill, that this was preconceived, premeditated killing, and that plan included the notion that the killer would cover the true intent or motive of the killing.

"And I think you can draw a logical inference that the killing itself, therefore, is a clue to the identity or motive of the perpetrator; and Dana Ewell is the obvious beneficiary of this killing. . . .

"The execution of these family members was committed with insider knowledge of the house and their goings-on. It's clear that the family arrives home at the perfect time to be executed.

"The executioner is lying in wait, the alarm system is off, there's no forced entry. This is, again looking at the circumstances, not a chance killing, but a lie-in-wait execution of a wealthy family.

"Dana Ewell has about seven or eight million reasons to want to kill his parents . . . " Oppliger said.

Dana Ewell and Joel Radovcich, said Oppliger, should be held to answer for the murders of Dale, Glee, and Tiffany Ewell.

47

"All right," said Judge Papadakis, "it appearing to the court the offenses alleged in the complaint having been committed, there being sufficient cause to believe defendants Dana James Ewell and Joel Patrick Radovcich guilty thereof, they're to be held to answer to the same."

The hearing was over. Both Dana and Joel would be tried on three counts of murder in the first degree, with the additional special circumstances of committing the murders for money, and lying-in-wait—sufficient, if convicted, to put them both in the gas chamber.

It would be more than eighteen months, at the earliest, before the case could come to a trial by jury—if it ever did. Already, the defense was erecting new obstacles to conviction.

For one, Terrence Woolf's destroy-the-defense-in-order-to-save-it strategy would soon come into play. He was removed as defense counsel and replaced by another lawyer, Phillip Cherney, who promptly filed a motion to dismiss the case against Joel Radovcich on the grounds that Joel had the ineffective assistance of counsel.

Similarly, Jones asked that charges be dropped against Dana because the double hearsay evidence was improperly accepted; without that tainted evidence, there was no evidence at all against Dana, Jones said, and so the case should be dismissed entirely.

When those efforts failed at the trial court level, Jones and Cherney appealed to the State Court of Appeals; simultaneously they began digging new entrenchments around their clients.

As expected, Jones demanded that Dana's case be tried separately from Joel's. The possibility was growing, based on the evidence, that Dana would be forced to accuse Joel of acting on his own, or in concert with Jack Ponce. The last thing Cherney and Joel needed was to have to face accusations not only from the District Attorney's office, but also from Dana and Jones.

And beyond those efforts, Jones and Cherney sought to have the records of the telephone calls and pager contacts thrown out, along with the financial records, arguing that the detectives had recklessly abused the truth in getting the still-sealed search warrants; and that items taken from the Ewell house after the murders had been improperly seized.

Was it all just technicalities, the last-ditch efforts of two desperate defendants to use the spins and curves of the law to get off, to escape their just deserts? Or was it, in the case of Dana Ewell at least, a sincere effort to avoid being convicted of a horrible crime that he had not committed?

Sometimes, watching Joel Radovcich in his plastic sandals and his maroon jail jumper, shackled hand and foot as he sat at the table during the long, interminable hearings over the following months, it seemed that Joel had already left the land of the living. He sat quietly, rarely moving, staring toward the ceiling. Occasionally, tremors would pass over his body, as if he were in some sort of trance.

What was Joel thinking? Did that pen-drawn image of the head exploding emanate from his imagination, or from reality? Did he wake up in the middle of the night on his hard jail bunk, seeing bits of bone and blood flying, bodies falling, three people dying by his own hand?

Was there a God?

And Dana. He sat at the table, two lawyers removed from

his former friend, likewise shackled. He followed the proceedings intently, occasionally whispering to Jones; there was little that happened in the courtroom that he did not quickly follow.

What were Dana's nights like? Were they filled with bitter outrage at the injustice of being locked up, cut off from his family, accused of a crime that he did not commit, driven by unbelievable circumstance into the arms of the very socialistic state he so despised?

Or was this just the biggest gamble of all?

Watching Dana, it was hard to fathom what was going on inside—to contemplate just what it was that had brought him to this place of ultimate jeopardy.

Here indeed was someone who had had all the advantages: wealth, certainly, and plenty of it; good looks; a first-class brain, a quality education; and parents who, by all accounts, indulged his every whim. How had this happened? If Dana Ewell was the prime mover of the events that cost his own family their lives, where and when was the seed of evil planted?

Was it rooted in the soil of Ohio farm country, where small greeds abode, from matters as trivial as tricks with saws, where every advantage was taken and ruthless ambition was the wellspring of determination?

Did it grow and ripen on the small airfields of Fresno, where the hustling of planes became an obsession, where money fueled the prodigious ascent of a man whose human values slowly withered and died, for whom winning became the only reality?

Did it flower in the abnormal atmosphere of a household that seemed strained by its insoluble contradictions between public and private behavior, where the image became the reality, and where there were no acts that had irretrievable consequences, so long as the image was maintained?

There is a clue to the puzzle, discernible in the assessment of Dana Ewell offered by Sean Shelby in the days immediately following the discovery of the murders. Shelby, Dana's friend, told the story of the time in junior high school, when the teacher asked students to think of the fastest way to get rich, and Dana was supposed to have replied, "Kill your parents."

It was only much later that detectives learned that Shelby had never been in the classroom with Dana; none of the students who were in the class recalled Dana making any such statement, even in jest. It was an apocryphal anecdote, a product of the image that had been rendered, not a reality.

Yet the very fact that such a thing could be said about Dana, and be believed, told more about Dana Ewell than twenty thousand pages of police reports, scientific tests, interviews, and photographs. Dale Ewell had been a ruthless, grasping man; his son, the anecdote seemed to say, was everything Dale had been, and more.

Here, if the charges were true, was the new model Ewell: Generation X out of nihilism, by way of the Greed Decade; cynical, self-centered, demanding, morally solipsistic, blinded by the illusory, if trendy, "paradox philosophy," where black was white and white was black, depending on how one cooked the books. Mothers, fathers, sisters, and grandmothers—in the new game all were expendable, assets to be downsized to maximize return. If the seed was planted in Ohio, it bore its poisonous fruit in a time of inhuman madness.